Human Resource Management
DeMYSTiFieD®

DeMYSTiFieD® Series

Accounting Demystified

Advanced Statistics Demystified

Algebra Demystified

Alternative Energy Demystified

ASP.NET 2.0 Demystified

Biology Demystified

Biotechnology Demystified

Business Calculus Demystified

Business Math Demystified

Business Statistics Demystified

C++ Demystified

Calculus Demystified

Chemistry Demystified

Commodities Demystified

Corporate Finance Demystified, 2e

Data Structures Demystified

Databases Demystified, 2e

Differential Equations Demystified

Digital Electronics Demystified

Electricity Demystified

Electronics Demystified

Environmental Science Demystified

Everyday Math Demystified

Financial Accounting Demystified

Financial Planning Demystified

Financial Statements Demystified

Forensics Demystified

Genetics Demystified

Grant Writing Demystified

Hedge Funds Demystified

Human Resource Management Demystified

Intermediate Accounting Demystified

Investing Demystified, 2e

Java Demystified

JavaScript Demystified

Lean Six Sigma Demystified

Linear Algebra Demystified

Macroeconomics Demystified

Management Accounting Demystified

Marketing Demystified

Math Proofs Demystified

Math Word Problems Demystified

Mathematica Demystified

Matlab Demystified

Microbiology Demystified

Microeconomics Demystified

Nanotechnology Demystified

OOP Demystified

Operating Systems Demystified

Options Demystified

Organic Chemistry Demystified

Pharmacology Demystified

Physics Demystified

Physiology Demystified

Pre-Algebra Demystified

Precalculus Demystified

Probability Demystified

Project Management Demystified

Public Speaking and Presentations Demystified

Quality Management Demystified

Real Estate Math Demystified

Robotics Demystified

Sales Management Demystified

Six Sigma Demystified, 2e

SQL Demystified

Statistical Process Control Demystified

Statistics Demystified

Technical Analysis Demystified

Technical Math Demystified

Trigonometry Demystified

UML Demystified

Visual Basic 2005 Demystified

Visual C# 2005 Demystified

XML Demystified

The Demystified Series publishes over 125 titles in all areas of academic study. For a complete list of titles, please visit www.mhprofessional.com.

Human Resource Management
DeMYSTiFieD®

Robert G. DelCampo

New York   Chicago   San Francisco   Lisbon   London   Madrid   Mexico City
New Delhi   San Juan   Seoul   Singapore   Sydney   Toronto

1 2 3 4 5 6 7 8 9 10 DOC/DOC 1 9 8 7 6 5 4 3 2 1 0

ISBN 978-0-07-173724-1
MHID   0-07-173724-3

This publication is designed to provide accurate and authoritative information in regard to the subject matter covered. It is sold with the understanding that neither the author nor the publisher is engaged in rendering legal, accounting, securities trading, or other professional services. If legal advice or other expert assistance is required, the services of a competent professional person should be sought.

> —*From a Declaration of Principles Jointly Adopted by a Committee of the American Bar Association and a Committee of Publishers and Associations*

Library of Congress Cataloging-in-Publication Data

DelCampo, Robert G.
  Human resource management demystified / by Robert G. DelCampo.
      p. cm.
  ISBN 978-0-07-173724-1 (alk. paper)
  1. Personnel management. I. Title.
  HF5549.D43612 2011
  658.3–dc22   2010038170

This book is printed on acid-free paper.

For Derek, Stephanie, Mom, and Dad
Thanks for all your love and support

About the Author

Robert G. DelCampo is an associate professor in the Department of Organization Studies at the University of New Mexico, holding the Rutledge Endowed Professorship in Management. He currently serves as editor-in-chief of *Administrative Sciences* and as associate editor of the *Business Journal of Hispanic Research* and was recently named to *New Mexico Business Weekly*'s "40 under 40" list of top young professionals and as one of *Albuquerque The Magazine*'s "15 People Who Will Change Albuquerque." He has consulted for more than 25 Fortune 500 companies, including Ford, Home Depot, Dell, and Intel. Rob earned a Ph.D. from the W. P. Carey School of Business at Arizona State University in Tempe, Arizona, in 2004, and holds MBA and undergraduate degrees from the University of New Mexico in Albuquerque.

Contents

Introduction

This book is for anyone who works for a company, for him- or herself, or for a small business, or who owns his or her own business. All too often, human resource management (HRM) is dismissed as "touchy-feely" or "soft people stuff"; it is rarely viewed as a valuable, trainable skill.

Most of the time, a skilled laborer, accountant, engineer, or "enter your original job title here" is promoted to "manager" or "area coordinator" on the basis of his or her skills in a particular functional area—OK, but now what? An excellent accountant or engineer may have no skills, knowledge, or training in managing people! So how do these folks acquire the appropriate managerial skills? Well, the reality is that some of them never do—they continue the process of trial and error in order to figure out "how things work" in their organization.

Human Resource Management DeMYSTiFieD serves as a starting point for these individuals. This text is not intended to be a substitute for formal HR training, but it is a jumping-off point, allowing individuals to realize the multi-faceted and essential skills that are taught to human resource managers. Like it or not, as individuals progress up the corporate ladder, sooner or later they will *need* to have some knowledge of HR. While some HR skills are innate (relating to other people, understanding their needs, and picking up on worker cues), others require extensive training. For instance, in the ever-changing legal landscape of the United States, who is in a protected class? Why? What does this mean? This is just one question of many from a seemingly endless list that are routinely asked of HR specialists.

In my experience educating HR professionals, I find that all too often there is adversarial relationship between HR and employees—HR is viewed as the enemy, or as being "on the side of management." What usually ends up happening is that

HR is ostracized by managers as being too employee-focused to be considered management, but housed in "corporate" and therefore not trusted by employees. In reality, however, HR *should* act as an advocate for employees to management, with no allegiance to anyone or anything except the best interests of the employee and of the organization overall. Hopefully, through exposure to the true function of HR, some of the misunderstandings about its role can be tempered.

The importance of human resources is immeasurable. I am constantly contacted by former students who chose to major in functional areas like finance, accounting, operations management, or marketing who tell me, "I only wish I had taken more HR and organizational behavior courses when I was in school!" They go on to say that these are the skills that can help them move up the corporate ladder and that specific functional skills vary so much from company to company that their skill set in finance, accounting, or some other such area must be retrained to the specific systems used by their company almost constantly. Relating to people and their needs, however, is a universal skill that is valued and desired by all organizations.

In Part I of this text, we discuss some of the basics of HR and some of the legal constraints placed on HR. In Part II, the specifics of determining what type and number of "human resources" are needed in your organization is covered. Part III then discusses what to do with these "resources" once they have been hired. HR departments often stress recruiting and hiring, but then once the employees reach the organization, they are left with little direction and structure.

It is my hope that at the end of this very introductory human resource self-teaching course, readers will all have a greater appreciation for, and understanding of, the need for well-trained human resource professionals. In today's business world, HR is often the first department to be outsourced or downsized, even though it actually can contain the most valuable workers in your organization!

How to Use This Book

In order to learn human resource management, you *must* have an open mind. While the application of human resource theory and law is relatively objective, on occasion you may be called upon to make a decision that contradicts your personal belief system. I am not referring to your ethical code of conduct, but perhaps you hold a deep political or spiritual belief that is not in accord with your organization's policies or U.S. law. In this case, you must fairly, and without bias, apply your knowledge of the extant theory and laws of human resources to the situation. Never compromise your ethical standards, but be prepared to make tough decisions.

This book contains an abundance of practice quiz, test, and exam questions. They are all multiple-choice, and they are similar to the sorts of questions used in standardized tests. There is a short quiz at the end of every chapter, and all of these quizzes are "open book." You may (and should) refer to the chapter texts when taking them. When you think you're ready, take the quiz, write down your answers, and then give your list of answers to a friend. The correct answers are given in the back of the book. Have your friend compare your answers to the correct ones and have him or her tell you your score, but not which questions you got wrong. Then repeat the quiz. Stick with a chapter until you get the majority of the answers right. A satisfactory score is answering three-quarters of the quiz correctly.

There is a final exam at the end of this book containing questions drawn from Parts I, II, and III. Take this exam when you have finished all the sections, all the section tests, and all the chapter quizzes. As with the chapter quizzes, ask a friend to compare the answers; if you have answered at least 75 percent of the questions correctly, this is a satisfactory score.

You might want to take each test, and the final exam, two or three times. When you have gotten a score that makes you happy, you can check to see where your knowledge is strong and where it is not so keen.

I recommend that you complete one chapter per sitting (an hour or two daily ought to be enough time for this). Don't rush yourself; give your mind time to absorb the material. But don't go too slowly, either. Take it at a steady pace and keep it up. That way, you'll complete the book's course in a reasonable amount of time. Then, when you're done, you can use this book and its comprehensive index as a permanent reference.

Part I

Overview and Compliance

chapter 1

HR in a Nutshell

This chapter presents an overview of human resource management (HRM), including its functions and its value to an organization. It also discusses more general functions of management and the unique value created by well-trained human resource professionals.

CHAPTER OBJECTIVES

After completing this chapter, the student should be able to

1. Understand the value of human resource management.
2. Identify the core functions of management.
3. Understand the varied forms of HR strategy.
4. Understand the fit between HR and firm strategy.

Functions of Management

First, let's review the four basic functions of management: (1) leading, (2) planning, (3) organizing, and (4) staffing. While HRM makes a significant contribution to each of these functions, traditionally, it has mainly dealt with the "staffing" aspect of an organization.

So what is meant by staffing? Well, lots of things, including conducting job analyses, planning labor needs, recruiting and selecting job candidates, orienting and training employees, managing wages and salaries, providing incentives to improve employee performance, managing benefits, facilitating communication between employees and managers, general and specific training, and developing and building employee commitment. That's an enormous list of responsibilities!

Still Struggling

The terms *HR* and *management* are sometimes used interchangeably, and you might also hear the terms *personnel* and *staffing* used for HR as well. It should be noted that human resource management is actually a distinct function of an organization, basically encompassing everything related to the humans (or "human resources") in your firm.

HR: Human Resources or Human Relations?

Often HR doesn't mean just human resources; it also means human *relations*. Think of the HR function as the umpire, adjudicating disputes among employees as well as between employees and management. More often than not, grievances about performance appraisals, promotions, hiring decisions, or other employment-related issues end up being handled by the organization's HR department. Therefore, communication is perhaps the most important of HR's responsibilities. However, before we look specifically at the roles of HR, let us consider how HR fits into the broader landscape of the organization.

So, what is the overall goal of management in an organization? To make money? To improve market share? To retain employees? To create a high-quality product or service? Perhaps, but superseding all of these is the goal of furthering the firm's chosen strategy. Therefore, in this book, we will look at HR through a strategic lens. Whether that strategy is to improve market position, improve market share, or maximize shareholder value, management's role is to use whatever resources are available to bring that strategy to fruition. The question then becomes, what is strategy, and how does HR fit into strategy?

Competitive advantage based on human talent has become essential in today's "war for talent." Human resource strategy is composed of, and advanced by, a set of HR tactics consisting of individual policies or programs that capitalize on competitive advantage for the firm as a whole. HR strategy is the conduit between HR tactics and the overall strategy of the firm. An HR strategy's effect on the firm's performance is always dependent on how well that strategy fits with other factors, and its success is dependent on the situation or context in which it is used. Key factors that firms should consider in determining which HR strategies will have a positive impact on the firm's performance include organizational strategies, environment, organizational characteristics, and organizational capabilities. Consistency among these variables dictates the success of a given firm's HR strategy.

 PROBLEM 1-1

List five examples showing how you used, or could have used, human resource management techniques at work or at school.

 SOLUTION

Examples include the following:
1. Improved the efficiency of work through the use of technology made available through human resource systems
2. Employed the services of nontraditional workers
3. Developed metrics to measure people's added value in terms of human resource contributions
4. Kept abreast of employment law in order to minimize risk to the company
5. Utilized self-service HR technology
6. Employed high-performance work systems concepts in the job

Challenges to HR

The human resource challenges that face today's managers may be categorized according to their primary focus: the environment, the organization, or the individual. Firms that deal with these challenges effectively are likely to out-perform those that do not.

First, the environmental challenges facing HR include rapid changes in the business environment; the diversity of the workforce; the growing need for a presence in the global marketplace; legislation by local, state, and federal governments; evolving work and family roles (workers needs and wants away from work); and, most important, shortages of skilled workers and the rise of the service sector.

HR faces several challenges within an organization as well. While the competitive position of the organization, decentralization of decision making, restructuring, and need for downsizing might seem salient, the constant battle with organizational higher-ups associated with such changes leave HR in constant flux. These challenges combined with ever-changing technology create significant obstacles to the creation of a coherent HR strategy and a well-functioning organization.

In addition to environmental and organizational challenges, there are also several individual challenges that human resource managers face. These include such things as appropriately matching people to the organization and clashing views about ethics and responsibility. In addition, productivity issues, brain drain, the attraction of a firm's most productive employees to competitors, and job insecurity of employees can all play a role.

HR is crucial to any organization's efficiency and health, and although there will always be challenges facing HR, selecting an appropriate HR strategy will allow HR to combat these issues, improve the effect of human resource management, and contribute to a more productive organization overall.

Still Struggling

Strategic HR is the process of linking your firm's strategy to the human resource function. This is an important connection, as many firms do not outsource or use "cookie-cutter" HR systems. Strategically focused human resource management can help your firm retain top talent and keep employees functioning at a high level.

Selecting HR Strategies

When selecting an HR strategy, it is of the utmost importance that organizational culture be the linchpin in determining how the strategy will be implemented. This social culture is made up of the assumptions and beliefs shared by the members of an organization, and also the organization's planned strategies.

Organizational strategies may be examined at two levels: corporate and business unit. Corporate strategy refers to the mix of businesses that a corporation decides to hold and the flow of resources among those businesses. This involves decisions pertaining to acquisitions, divestments, diversification, and growth. Business unit strategies refer to those strategies established by firms or autonomous units within the corporation. Well-known business strategies were formulated by Porter, Miles, and Snow.

A strong culture will create cohesion and similar thought processes throughout the company. So in a sense, organizational culture becomes the lens through which everyone in the organization interprets events, competitors, and the external environment. If the culture is opposed to change or to a particular HR strategy, how can HR overcome this resistance?

This is a question that HR managers face on a daily basis. First, HR managers must be in touch with the characteristics of their organization and its employees, and their capabilities, in order to choose consistent HR tactics that will allow them to successfully implement HR strategies. Next, HR strategies must align not only with organizational strategies, but also with the external environment and environmental opportunities, overall business strategies, and an organization's unique characteristics and distinctive competencies.

HR strategies should help the organization better exploit environmental opportunities or cope with the unique environmental forces that affect it. The environment can be examined on four dimensions: (1) degree of uncertainty, (2) volatility, (3) magnitude, and (4) complexity.

To be most effective, HR strategies must be tailored to the organization's personality. The features of an organization's personality are its (1) production process for converting inputs into output, (2) market posture, (3) overall managerial philosophy, (4) organizational structure, and (5) organizational culture.

An organization's capabilities are its distinct competencies. HR strategies make a greater contribution to a firm's performance (1) when they help to exploit the firm's specific advantages or strengths while avoiding its weaknesses, and (2) when they assist it in better using its own unique blend of human resource skills and assets.

A firm that has a poorly defined HR strategy or a business strategy that does not explicitly incorporate human resources is likely to lose ground to its competitors. Similarly, a firm may have a well-articulated HR strategy but still fail if its HR tactics and policies do not help it to implement its HR strategy effectively.

Formulating HR strategies and establishing programs to implement them is called *strategic human resource planning*. Successful strategic HR planning provides many benefits for the company, including (1) encouragement of proactive rather than reactive behavior, (2) explicit communication of company goals, (3) stimulation of critical thinking and ongoing examination of assumptions, (4) identification of gaps between the current situation and the future vision, (5) encouragement of line managers' participation, (6) identification of HR constraints and opportunities, and (7) creation of common bonds.

In developing HR strategies, organizations face several important challenges, including (1) maintaining a competitive advantage, (2) reinforcing overall business strategy, (3) avoiding excessive concentration on day-to-day problems, (4) developing HR strategies that are suited to unique organizational features, (5) coping with the environment, (6) securing management commitment, (7) translating the strategic plan into action, (8) combining intended and emergency strategies, and (9) accommodating change.

 **PROBLEM 1-2**

Develop several lists showing how trends like workforce diversity, technological trends, globalization, and changes in the nature of work have affected the organization where you currently work.

 SOLUTION

This list might include items such as
- **Growth of nontraditional student populations**
- **Use of computer/communication technology**
- **Diversity issues**

The options that a firm has available in designing its HR system are called *strategic HR choices*. No HR strategy is "good" or "bad" in and of itself. The success of HR strategies depends on the situation or context in which they are used.

In other words, an HR strategy's effect on a firm's performance is always dependent on how well it fits with some of the other factors affecting that firm. *Fit* refers to the consistency or compatibility between HR strategies and other important aspects of the organization.

Still Struggling

Strategic HR can itself be a vehicle for achieving higher levels of firm performance. While there is no one specific way to guarantee improved performance, the adage that "a happy worker is a productive worker" does ring true.

Even the best-laid strategic HR plans, however, may fail when specific HR programs are poorly chosen or implemented. A firm's HR strategies must be mutually consistent. That is, HR strategies are more likely to be effective if they reinforce one another rather than work at cross-purposes.

 PROBLEM 1-3

Contact the HR manager of a local business. Ask that person how he or she is working as a strategic partner to manage human resources given the firm's strategic goals and objectives.

 SOLUTION

You may be surprised to find how much impact HR has on strategy (either a great deal or in some cases none at all). Use this opportunity to discuss the bridge between theory and practice

All managers must be able to deal with human resource issues effectively because these issues are at the core of being a good manager. Moreover, mutual partnerships must be formed among line managers and HR professionals in order to meet the employees' and employer's goals and needs effectively and efficiently. It is not uncommon for managers and HR to view each other negatively, which often hinders the establishment of an effective partnership. Five competencies for human resource professionals are required if a human resource department is to become a full strategic partner: (1) leadership, (2) knowledge of the business, (3) HR strategic thinking, (4) process skills, and (5) HR technologies.

Specific steps that a company can take to foster an effective partnership between managers and the HR department include (1) analyzing the people side of productivity, (2) viewing HR professionals as internal consultants, (3) instilling a shared sense of common fate, (4) requiring some managerial experience, (5) actively involving top corporate and divisional managers, and (6) requiring senior HR executives to participate.

As you progress further in this text, you will see that each individual chapter discusses different HR tactics. Though the chapter titles may refer to separate tactics, it is important to note that we take a strategic approach when discussing each. As a self-teaching guide, *Human Resource Management DeMYSTiFieD* is designed to introduce professionals to the concepts behind human resource management through self-study in survey form. It is our hope that, by examining these concepts, practicing managers will gain working knowledge in each of these areas, thereby becoming more effective at making personnel decisions within their organizations.

 PROBLEM 1-4

Using the Internet or library sources, analyze the annual reports of at least five companies. Write down examples of how those companies say they are using their HR processes to help the company achieve its strategic goals.

 SOLUTION

How effective are the HR processes that each company is using to support its strategic goals? Try to come up with additional ideas for other approaches to using the HR processes and how each company would go about implementing them, noting the company's specific challenges.

Chapter Summary

Human resource management in today's organizations presents not only a series of challenges, but also a series of opportunities to capitalize on strengths. Think about the individual words—*human, resource,* and *management.* In sum, these terms dictate that *people* in *organizations* are *resources* that must be managed in order to optimize their value. This is the essence of human resource management—the people make the place. Throughout this text, we will discuss, evaluate, and emphasize the strategies and tactics that are necessary if today's managers are to maximize their people resources. In today's organizations, products change, production changes, and sales change, but people dictate whether or not your organization will be successful in the long-term. Rather than thinking of HRM as a series of difficult practices, procedures, and processes that must be followed or legal hurdles that must be jumped over in order to get things done, think of it as a way to retain valued employees and maintain the quality of the culture in your organization.

QUIZ

1. **Which of the following is not one of the four basic functions of management?**
   A. Staffing
   B. Leading
   C. Organizing
   D. Developing

2. **Human resources strategy is made up of**
   A. Organizational resources and capabilities that help a company gain strategic advantage over its competitors.
   B. A set of HR tactics that capitalize on competitive advantage for the firm as a whole.
   C. Key success factors in an industry that help a firm gain competitive advantage.
   D. Combining strategies throughout the organization and using HR tactics to gain competitive advantage.

3. **In HR management, evolving work and family roles is considered this type of challenge:**
   A. Individual
   B. Managerial
   C. Environmental
   D. Organizational

4. **Which key factors should firms consider in determining which HR strategies will have a positive impact on a firm's performance?**
   A. Organizational strategies, characteristics, capabilities, and the environment
   B. Organizational structure and systems
   C. Organizational resources and capabilities
   D. Organizational structure and competitor key success factors

5. **Which of the following is not one of the competencies required for an HR department to become a full strategic partner in an organization?**
   A. Performance management skills
   B. HR technologies
   C. Knowledge of the business
   D. HR strategic thinking

6. **In HR management, decentralization of decision making is considered this type of challenge:**
   A. Individual
   B. Managerial
   C. Environmental
   D. Organizational

7. **HR strategies must align with**
   A. Organizational strategic thinking.
   B. Organizational characteristics and capabilities.
   C. Both organizational strategies and the external environment.
   D. Organizational tactics and a strategic lens.

8. **To foster an effective partnership between managers and the HR department, companies can**
   A. Instill a shared sense of common fate.
   B. View HR professionals as external consultants.
   C. Invite departmental leaders to participate.
   D. Analyze financial productivity.

9. **Corporate strategy can be defined as**
   A. Strategy among the established firms or units of the corporation.
   B. Organizational exploitation of leadership strategy, differentiation, and competitive advantage.
   C. The mix of businesses that a corporation decides to hold and the flow of resources among those businesses.
   D. Organizational strategic tactics to gain market share among competitors.

10. **In HR management, the existence of clashing views about ethics and responsibility is considered this type of challenge:**
    A. Individual
    B. Managerial
    C. Environmental
    D. Organizational

chapter 2

Equal Employment Opportunity (EEO) and the Law

This chapter provides a cursory description of the major pieces of legislation governing human resource policies in the United States of America. While this discussion is not intended to be exhaustive, knowing the major historical and current laws governing the hiring and treatment of employees is key to understanding the role of human resources in today's corporate environment.

CHAPTER OBJECTIVES

After completing this chapter, the student should be able to

1. Identify and understand the limitations of human resource management.
2. Understand the relationship between HR and the law.
3. Describe and conduct a *utilization analysis*.
4. Understand the provisions of the Americans with Disabilities Act, the Equal Pay Act, and the Civil Rights Act.
5. Understand the types of sexual harassment and the liability that sexual harassment poses.

Understanding the Legal Environment

Why is it important that you understand the legal environment that HR operates within? Well, for starters, you need this in order to "do the right thing" when it comes to making ethical decisions. Second, you need it so that managers can understand the limitations of the HR and legal departments, in turn protecting themselves from culpability. And lastly, you need it to limit potentially damaging public relations issues that could affect the company, both financially and in its reputation.

First, you need to look at the ethical implications—as a manager, you have to live with yourself and the decisions that you've made. Thus, making a decision that is in compliance with the law is essential, but one's ethical standards should also remain intact. In order to be sure that a decision is in accord with general ethical principles, it is important to ask yourself three questions:

1. Is the decision legal? If yes, proceed to question two.
2. Is the decision balanced—are both parties treated fairly and at least given equal consideration? If yes, proceed to question three.
3. How would someone I respect (parent, coworker, mentor, and so on) feel about this decision?

If you are comfortable with the answers to each of these questions, you can be fairly certain that you've made a legal, rational, and ethical decision. If not, perhaps you need to go back and reevaluate.

Second, it is important that you realize the limitations of the HR and legal departments within your organization. If managers make poor decisions, the HR department will not always be able to resolve the situation. For this reason, it is crucial that all managers have a working familiarity with HR, but additionally that the HR department is familiar with the legal constraints placed upon human resource functions by U.S. and state-level statutory requirements.

Finally, limiting potential liability is paramount for the HR function. Not only can there be financial consequences for doing something improperly (such as having a lawsuit filed against your firm for giving someone an unfair performance appraisal), but, perhaps even more important, the public relations ramifications can be tremendously severe. For example, several years ago, Denny's had an issue with negative publicity resulting from one of its restaurants not serving particular individuals because of their race. News of the incident was immediately carried by all major news venues, and Denny's public image was tarnished by the discriminatory actions of a small group of employees.

While this wasn't exactly an HR issue, more than likely it was the HR department that had to address the situation. While it is possible that the employees involved could be sanctioned, or perhaps that this particular location will lose its franchise, how is HR going to remedy this issue in the popular press? HR needs to consider that any employee in an organization operates as an agent of that organization. Employees carry the name of the organization with them, and their actions reflect the organization—whether they have been authorized to represent the organization or not. This "for better or for worse" quandary is often left for HR to manage and police. While it is difficult to control all the aspects of an employee's life, considering a potential employee's demeanor and temperament should be an important portion of the hiring process.

 PROBLEM 2-1

Why should managers be concerned with understanding human resource law instead of leaving it to the experts?

 SOLUTION

A firm's HR department has considerable responsibilities with respect to human resource law. However, if managers make poor decisions, the HR department will not always be able to resolve the situation. The manager's job is to prevent the damage from happening in the first place. Thus, understanding and complying with HR law helps the manager to do the right thing, realize the limitations of the HR and legal departments, and minimize potential liability.

Ideal Behavior and Affirmative Action

Some specific issues related to EEO and the legal environment include issues of ideal behavior versus affirmative action hiring practices. Inherently, many managers feel that they are facing an ethical dilemma when they are trying to decide between ideal behavior (making hiring decisions without paying any attention to race, ethnicity, or gender) and the use of affirmative action policies (which are intended to right previous wrongs by giving individuals opportunities that previously were not available to them as members of an underrepresented work group).

Ideal behavior works toward human resource practices built on seeking balance in making decisions with regard to traditionally underrepresented groups at work. Fair employment is the overall goal of all EEO legislation, as regulation is seen as a means of ensuring that employment decisions are unaffected by illegal discrimination. Unfortunately, discrimination in employment practices is part of American history. For this reason, affirmative action, while not a law, is a policy used by government organizations and government contractors for the purpose of limiting the present effects of past discrimination. While this policy is controversial, it is important for you as HR professionals to explore your personal feelings and what you've heard about these policies. Once you have established your own beliefs, you can buffer your reaction and reconcile the law and your organization's policies realistically. In theory, affirmative action is designed to "level the playing field" and allow individuals who have not had opportunities in the past (including such things as access to education) to achieve higher-level positions in a variety of organizations.

Ideal behavior and affirmative action are considered to be competing strategies, but both work toward fair employment in society as a whole. It seems that everyone—firms, government contractors, employees, and even courts of law—has different views regarding the best way to achieve equitable HR treatment. One method of limiting the potential for discriminatory hiring is to create an action plan in which a utilization analysis, which describes the organization's current workforce relative to the qualified workers in the labor force, is performed. This analysis is often called an *availability analysis*. The first step in this action plan is to determine the demographic composition of your current workforce. The second step is to determine the percentage of your targeted demographic in the firm's available labor market. Important factors to consider in this process are

- *The local population.* It's important to determine what the population of your local environment or the constituencies served by the organization look like demographically. An effective firm staffs its organization to match its primary constituency.

- *Local unemployed workers.* What percentage of the labor market targeted is unemployed? Are there enough available qualified applicants?

- *The local labor force.* Who makes up the local labor force? What are the typical job titles? What are the typical job functions of people in this labor force?

- *Qualified workers in the local labor market.* Who are the qualified workers in your local labor market? Are they spread across the spectrum of races, ethnicities, and genders? What percentage has the proper education/certification and other such qualifications?

- *Current employees.* Who from inside your organization can be considered? Look at the current composition of your workforce; who possesses the necessary skills, knowledge, or abilities to move into higher-level jobs within the organization?

- *Graduates of local education and training programs.* How many are available in your constituency? How have they been trained, and when will they be ready to take on these jobs? What is the demographic composition of these graduates?

- *Training programs sponsored by employers.* Many times, employers will take on individuals from diverse demographic groups and train them in order to fill a need for people who fit a particular demographic profile. Does your organization currently participate in any such training programs?

Think about the local population of the area in which your organization functions. What is the percentage of ethnic minorities? What is the percentage of college-educated people? How many people are below the poverty line? Where has there been growth in the past few years? All of these questions need to be considered by HR when hiring. To help in doing so, HR will perform what is called an *availability analysis.* By doing this sort of analysis, organizations can determine what their workforce should look like if it is to be representative of the population it serves. This could also be considered creating a stratified sample of sorts of the population served by the organization and then mirroring the organizational demographics to that population.

PROBLEM 2-2

What three steps are involved in developing an affirmative action program? How much flexibility does an employer have in developing the specific points in such a program?

SOLUTION

The three steps involved in developing an affirmative action program are (1) conducting a utilization analysis, (2) establishing goals and timetables, and (3) determining action options. In the first step, organizations need to consider multiple pieces of information, which constitute an availability analysis, after they have conducted a utilization analysis. In the second step, the Office of Federal Contract Compliance Programs (OFCCP) explicitly requires that rigid numerical quotas not be set. Rather, the employer should take into consideration the size of the underutilization, how fast

the workforce turns over, and whether the workforce is growing or contracting. In the third step, the OFCCP suggests that companies recruit protected-class members, redesign jobs, provide specialized training, and remove unnecessary employment barriers.

Discrimination

Although we would like to think that discrimination has been eradicated from the U.S. workforce, the truth is that it still exists. While we are all familiar with discrimination based on gender, race, ethnicity, religion, age, and sexual preference, what might be surprising are some other bases of discrimination that are not currently the subject of legislation, such as pregnancy, manner of dress, grooming, hair color or style, attractiveness, whether or not potential employees smoke, and level of health. While these types of discrimination are not legislated against, they have become issues in the popular press in recent years. Therefore, when an organization is hiring, the following questions need to be asked with regard to these issues: How should they be dealt with? Are we always cognizant of the biases that we have when making decisions? How do we draw the line between discrimination and making a smart decision for our organization? These can be difficult questions to answer, ones that HR departments have to wrestle with on a regular basis.

Antidiscrimination Legislation

The Americans with Disabilities Act of 1990

The Americans with Disabilities Act of 1990 (ADA) is a law designed to limit employment discrimination against individuals with disabilities who are otherwise able to perform the essential functions of a job, with or without reasonable accommodation. Specific definitions of "reasonable" and "essential" are left to the interpretation of the employer or, ultimately, decided by litigation. However, the cost of "reasonable accommodation" can range from minimal (it has been reported that one-third of all reasonable accommodation is at zero cost to the employer) to extreme, and what is reasonable is regularly litigated in the American court system.

The act provides an opportunity for individuals with disabilities who can perform essential job functions to work in various organizations. It's important to note that the ADA does not apply to organizations with 15 or fewer employees. This exception is to protect family-owned and small businesses that may be incapable, unable, or unwilling to incur the sometimes high costs of making reasonable accommodations for employees with disabilities.

The Civil Rights Act of 1964

Many people credit the passage of the Civil Rights Act of 1964 to the open, explosive discrimination based on race that was being experienced at the time. Title VII of the Civil Rights Act of 1964 is universally seen as the most important civil rights law passed to date. The act itself has several sections, all of which are aimed at prohibiting discrimination in various parts of society. Title VII of the act states the following:

Section 703. (a) Employer practices

It shall be an unlawful employment practice for an employer—

(1) to fail or refuse to hire or to discharge any individual, or otherwise to discriminate against any individual with respect to his compensation, terms, conditions, or privileges of employment, because of such individual's race, color, religion, sex, or national origin; or

(2) to limit, segregate, or classify his employees or applicants for employment in any way which would deprive or tend to deprive any individual of employment opportunities or otherwise adversely affect his status as an employee, because of such individual's race, color, religion, sex, or national origin.

As you can see, Title VII of the Civil Rights Act includes many of the traditional bases of discrimination, but neglects to mention discrimination against a number of other diverse groups.

Equal Pay Act of 1963

The Equal Pay Act of 1963 states that women and men will be given equal pay for work that is "substantially similar." The Bureau of Labor Statistics shows that men and women working in similar jobs do not receive equal pay: women earn between $0.72 and $0.87 for each dollar earned by men. While such differences should not be tolerated, it is important to note that this pay gap has been closing over the past few years, even though the rate at which it has been doing so still lags behind the rates in other industrialized nations. While many argue about the limitations of this act, and whether it truly does affect salaries for men and women, such legislation helps establish cases in which discrimination based on gender truly exists.

Age Discrimination in Employment Act, 1967

In 1967, the Age Discrimination in Employment Act was passed. This act protects individuals over the age of 40 from discrimination based on their age. The act established those over the age of 40 as a protected class. Interestingly, younger employees (those under 40) who might routinely be ostracized for their lack of experience or "new approaches" to business cannot claim discrimination based on their age.

Still Struggling

In most cases, large firms will rely on the attorneys to interpret and apply relevant employment law. While the description of these laws has been simplified here, the laws have many nuances and intricacies. If you are confused, that is fine: an entire industry of employment lawyers exists to serve as a resource for you and your firm!

Types of Discrimination

Two types of discrimination are generally recognized: *disparate treatment* and *adverse impact*.

Disparate treatment is direct discrimination resulting from unequal treatment and occurs when an employer treats an employee differently because of his or her status as a member of a protected class. This type of discrimination typically involves race or sex and is considered intentional, based on prejudiced actions leading to different groups being held to different standards.

Adverse impact (also called *disparate impact*) is indirect discrimination. It occurs when the same standards are applied to all applicants or employees, even if one or more of these standards affect a protected class negatively. Unequal consequences or results for members of minority groups therefore occur. For example, people of different racial backgrounds or genders receive different treatment that is often unintentional, yet still discriminatory. In this situation, apparently neutral actions require the same standards but result in different consequences for different groups. For example, a test was given to determine who would receive a particular promotion within a company: 80 percent of the men taking the test passed it, but 80 percent of the women failed. Based on such results, one might contend that this test was gender-biased, as it may not have accurately reflected the ability of each applicant.

Equal Employment Opportunity Commission (EEOC) Definition of Harassment

The 1980 definition of sexual harassment differs greatly from the 1993 definition used today. The 1980 definition reads as follows:

> Unwelcome sexual advances, requests for sexual favors, and other verbal or physical conduct of a sexual nature constitute sexual harassment when:
>
> 1. Submission to such conduct is made either explicitly or implicitly a term or condition of an individual's employment;
> 2. Submission to or rejection of such conduct by an individual is used as a basis for employment decisions affecting such individual; or
> 3. Such conduct has the purpose or effect of unreasonably interfering with an individual's work performance or creating an intimidating, hostile, or offensive working environment.

The 1980 definition was only an interpretation of the law, not an amendment to the Title VII sex-based discrimination legislation already in existence. As you can see, the 1993 definition of harassment issued by the EEOC is vastly different from that more general 1980 description. The more inclusive 1993 description has increased the number of cases filed, not only with regard to sexual harassment, but also with regard to harassment based on factors such as race, age, and disabilities.

Unlawful harassment is verbal or physical conduct that denigrates or shows hostility or aversion toward an individual because of his or her race, color, religion, gender, national origin, age or disability, or that of his/her relatives, friends, or associates, and that:

1. has the purpose or effect of creating an intimidating, hostile, or offensive working environment;

2. has the purpose or effect of unreasonably interfering with an individual's work performance; or

3. otherwise adversely affects an individual's employment opportunities.

The EEOC's altering of the definition of harassment has resulted in two different types of sexual harassment being claimed in today's workforce. The first is *quid pro quo sexual harassment*, also known as "something for something." In this instance, a one-to-one exchange of some sort of favor is demanded in return for a desired outcome with regard to hiring, promotion, salary improvement, or any type of advancement or special treatment within an organization. The second type of harassment is called *hostile environment sexual harassment*. This type would include groups of employees charging their employer with creating a hostile work environment. The Supreme Court has listed four questions to help judges and juries decide whether verbal or other behavior of a sexual nature creates a hostile work environment: (1) How frequent is the discriminatory conduct? (2) How severe is the discriminatory conduct? (3) Is the conduct physically threatening or humiliating? (4) Does the conduct interfere with the employee's work performance?

It is important to note that hostile work environment claims are much more difficult to prove than quid pro quo claims.

So how does an organization go about reducing its potential liability in the realm of sexual harassment? Managers should be aware of recent U.S. Supreme Court sexual harassment rulings that directly affect employer liability in sexual harassment cases. For example, an employer may be held liable for the actions of supervisors toward their subordinate employees, even if the offense is not reported to top management.

The Supreme Court has also established an employer defense against sexual harassment claims. The employer must prove two items: (1) The employer exercised reasonable care to prevent and correct sexual harassment problems in a timely manner, and (2) the plaintiff failed to use the internal procedures for reporting sexual harassment. In order to meet these criteria in a court of law, it would be in the employer's best interests to:

- Establish a written policy prohibiting harassment.
- Communicate the policy and train employees in what constitutes harassment.
- Establish an effective complaint procedure.
- Quickly investigate all claims.
- Take remedial action to correct past harassment.
- Make sure that the complainant does not end up in a less desirable position if he or she needs to be transferred.
- Follow up to prevent continued harassment.

 PROBLEM 2-3

"Sexual harassment is a problem that occurs between two employees. The company should not be held liable for the actions of misbehaving employees." Do you agree or disagree with this statement? Explain your answer.

 SOLUTION

While some people may agree with this statement, from a human resources, as well as a legal, perspective, the correct response is to disagree. Sexual harassment is a major EEO issue for employers. Recent U.S. Supreme Court sexual harassment rulings have directly affected employers' liability in sexual harassment cases. Particularly in cases of supervisor/subordinate relationships, an employer may be held liable for the actions of supervisors toward their subordinate employees even if the offense is not reported to top management.

In a recent ruling, the Supreme Court has established an employer defense against sexual harassment claims. The employer must prove that (1) it exercised reasonable care to prevent and correct sexual harassment problems in a timely manner, and (2) the plaintiff failed to use the internal procedures for reporting sexual harassment. To safeguard against sexual harassment claims, it is recommended that employers develop a zero-tolerance sexual harassment policy, successfully communicate the policy to employees, and ensure that victims can report abuses without fear of retaliation.

Addressing EEO Complaints

There are three main options that exist for employers and employees who are facing EEO complaints:

1. *Litigation.* Employment discrimination claims represent the largest number of civil rights suits filed annually in federal courts.
2. *Arbitration.* This is less costly, and arbitrators are not bound to abide by prevailing laws.
3. *Internal dispute resolution.* This is still less costly and is handled by entities within the company (up the chain of control).

HR professionals should be familiar with the benefits and potential costs of each option. In all cases, it should be noted that employees and employers should aim to reach an equitable outcome in the shortest time period with the most efficient method.

Resources for Further Information

It's important to evaluate what current information is available in the ever-changing landscape of EEO regulations. Please feel free to get in contact with the following government agencies for additional details.

- Equal Employment Opportunity Commission (EEOC): http://www.eeoc.gov
- Office of Federal Contract Compliance Programs (OFCCP): http://www.dol.gov/elaws/ofccp

 **PROBLEM 2-4**

Suppose you are a plant manager and one of your employees has trouble controlling his anger; he experiences wide swings in emotions as a result of bipolar disorder (a medical condition). You are aware that he has been under the treatment of a psychiatrist. This employee recently threatened other employees with violence, and you have placed him on leave until his psychiatrist indicates to you that his emotional condition has stabilized. Can the angry employee use the ADA to obtain a reasonable accommodation and get reinstated in his job or a modified one? What further information would you need, if any, to assess this issue?

 **SOLUTION**

Sure, the employee can use the ADA to obtain a reasonable accommodation. The question is whether or not there is a reasonable accommodation that can be made. Employers are not required to risk the safety and health of their other employees in order to accommodate an ADA claim. However, if there is an accommodation that can be made that will keep all employees safe, it should be made.

The following questions should be asked to obtain useful information regarding this situation: Are there specific types of situations or incidents that "set the employee off"? Are there environments or times of day that contribute to the incidents? Is the employee actually violent? Has he ever actually acted on his emotions? Does the employee or his psychiatrist have any suggestions for accommodations?

Chapter Summary

For HR managers, EEO and the law are two of the most important considerations in decision making. It should be noted that understanding legal requirements in recruiting, interviewing, and hiring employees is the responsibility of everyone who is involved in the process, but this is also an area in which using good judgment and asking the firm's legal department (or outside counsel) for help are always positive ideas. In today's litigious society, you can never be too careful when making any sort of personnel decision. If something seems questionable, do not hesitate to contact an expert or colleague to make sure that you are in compliance with both company policy and the law.

QUIZ

1. The Age Discrimination in Employment Act of 1967 protects individuals of or older than
   A. 30.
   B. 35.
   C. 40.
   D. 45.

2. Which is not one of the three main reasons for complying with HR law?
   A. It helps the company do the right thing.
   B. HR law sides with employers in nearly all situations.
   C. It allows the company to recognize the limitations of the HR and legal departments.
   D. Doing so limits potential liability.

3. Title VII of the Civil Rights Act of 1964 mandates that employment decisions may not be based on which of the following?
   A. Race, color, religion, sex, sexual orientation, or national origin
   B. Race, color, religion, ethnicity, sex, sexual orientation, or national origin
   C. Race, color, religion, sex, or national origin
   D. Race, color, ethnicity, sex, sexual orientation, or national origin

4. The Equal Pay Act of 1963 requires that
   A. Men and women are paid equally for similar work in all like organizations.
   B. Men and women receive the same pay if they do the same job in the same organization.
   C. Individuals receive similar pay for jobs within a similar grade of the organization.
   D. Individuals of a protected class are paid equally for similar work in all like organizations.

5. ABC Inc. uses an employment test that seems to screen out a disproportionate number of young Asian American women. If true, this would be an example of
   A. The four-fifths rule.
   B. Adverse impact.
   C. Disparate treatment.
   D. Unequal treatment.

6. Quid pro quo sexual harassment can best be defined in the following way:
   A. The employee is required to engage in sexual activity in exchange for workplace entitlements or benefits.
   B. Harassment is unwelcome by the harassed person and becomes sufficiently severe or pervasive to create an abusive environment.

    C. An organization fails to require sexual harassment training for its employees and an incident occurs.

    D. Two parties willingly engage in sexual activity in the workplace.

7. **Which statement is true about quotas?**

    A. The percentage of women and/or minorities that an organization must hire to correct underrepresentation is based on availability in the geographic area.

    B. Employers must make a good faith effort to fulfill quotas set by their affirmative action plan.

    C. Employers are required to hire a person who helps them to reach a placement goal, whether or not there is a more qualified candidate.

    D. They are expressly forbidden.

8. **What form of sexual harassment exists when an employee suffers job loss or experiences unfavorable personnel action for not complying with demands for favors?**

    A. Adverse impact

    B. Quid pro quo

    C. Hostile environment

    D. Disparate treatment

9. **Disparate treatment can be defined as**

    A. Treating similarly situated employees differently because of prohibited Title VII factors.

    B. The effect of facially neutral policy is deleterious to a Title VII group.

    C. Using a screening device to weed out applicants from the pool of candidates.

    D. An employer having been found to have intentionally discriminated against a specific candidate for no apparent reason.

10. **Suppose 100 women and 100 men take a promotion examination. If 100 percent of the men and 50 percent of the women pass the exam, what type of discrimination has occurred?**

    A. Adverse impact

    B. Disparate treatment

    C. Direct discrimination

    D. Indirect discrimination

Diversity in Organizations

This chapter covers the importance of diversity in today's workforce. Rather than simply focusing on racioethnic and gender differences, we describe the benefits and pitfalls faced by HR professionals in their efforts to diversify their workforce.

CHAPTER OBJECTIVES

After completing this chapter, the student should be able to

1. Describe the nature of diversity in today's workforce.

2. Identify challenges to managing employee diversity.

3. Understand the available options for improving diversity management.

4. Understand the difference between affirmative action and the management of diversity.

What Is Diversity?

Diversity simply refers to human characteristics that make people different. The sources of individual variations are complex, but they can generally be grouped into two categories: those over which individuals have little or no control, and those over which individuals have at least some or more control. Today's conception of diversity involves more than just gender, race, religion, and country of origin and includes factors such as educational background, functional area, communication style, and other individual differences.

Diversity is considered to be an asset in terms of improving organizational functioning and reflecting the customer market. Managing diversity is an outgrowth of natural or environmental trends such as demographic changes and international competition. Unless it is effectively managed, diversity among employees may have a negative impact on productive teamwork.

When considering diversity in the workplace, it must be pointed out that affirmative action is not diversity management. Furthermore, affirmative action is *not* the law—it is a policy enacted to help right past wrongs. The policy emerged from government pressure on businesses to provide greater opportunities for women and minorities. While U.S. government contractors are required to have affirmative action policies, private companies can make their own decisions about how to address this issue.

Still Struggling

Diversity is often portrayed as being essential for a high-functioning organization. While this is important, you should still go into it with your eyes open—along with people with varied backgrounds, experience, and values also come opportunities for conflict.

Why Manage Employee Diversity?

Current population trends dictate the available and qualified members of the labor pool in today's ever-changing population. Therefore, management of diversity is becoming essential in creating a competitive organization. Diverse employees bring unique thoughts, actions, skill sets, and approaches to what can sometimes be monotonous tasks. It should be noted that "diversity for diversity's sake" should never be a hiring strategy. Instead, managers should strategically determine the areas of deficiency within their organization and what sorts of employees might bring unique perspectives to the organization.

 PROBLEM 3-1

Conflicts among minority groups may arise as they compete for what they perceive as a limited number of jobs and promotion opportunities. Is this perception accurate? What can firms do to avoid these kinds of conflict?

 SOLUTION

Yes, most people would agree that this perception is accurate. As minorities within the U.S. population grow both proportionately and absolutely, competition among them for jobs and opportunities is likely to become much stronger. There already are rising tensions among minorities that are jockeying for advancement, and employers are being put into the uncomfortable position of having to decide which minority is most deserving.

There are no foolproof techniques for handling these challenges effectively. There is, however, one principle that managers should keep in mind: treat employees as individuals, not as members of a group. With this principle as a guide, many of these challenges become much more manageable.

Managing employee diversity is quite different from affirmative action. Affirmative action programs were designed to provide opportunities for qualified members of traditionally underrepresented groups. This does *not* mean dictating a lower standard for these individuals. Instead, an affirmative action policy provides preferential treatment to members of protected classes should two candidates be equally qualified.

For example, Candidate A and Candidate B are judged to be identical in their ability to work at XYZ Company. However, Candidate A is an Asian American female, while Candidate B is a white male. Since Candidate A is a member of a traditionally underrepresented group, XYZ's affirmative action policy would dictate that she be hired.

Of course, problems arise when firms misapply the tenets of affirmative action—which is quite easy to do. Think about it: are two candidates ever *exactly* identical? No. So it is rather naïve to think that affirmative action can be applied in every case. Misapplication of affirmative action policies by giving preferential treatment to members of traditionally underrepresented groups is common.

PROBLEM 3-2

What ethical problems might arise as a result of giving certain employees preferential treatment based on their group membership?

SOLUTION

There are many ethical problems that could arise. The most evident is the belief that by giving preferential treatment to anybody based on issues other than job performance, you are being unfair and acting unethically. This could have an impact on an organization's bottom line (because of lower performance), morale, and employee retention.

The concept of managing diversity goes beyond affirmative action. This process has many facets, including, but not limited to, matching the makeup of your organization to that of the population you serve. For example, as the fastest-growing minority group in the United States, Hispanics wield billions of dollars in purchasing power. As a result, might it make sense to have Hispanics in one's organization to enable it to market to that group effectively? Of course! But it should be noted that hiring *only* Hispanics could also create a problem. Overall, having a workforce with diverse backgrounds based on racioethnicity, education, functional area, or other such factors is essential to having a creative, effective, and innovative organization.

Creating an inclusive organization is also one of the most cost-effective and easily implemented methods of increasing productivity and employee morale, while improving the public relations image of the firm. Add this to the fact that creating a properly represented work group is simply an ethically "right thing to do," and diversity can become a corporate cornerstone of almost any organization, big or small. The advantages of diversifying one's workforce are similar to the advantages of diversifying one's personal assets. Would you want 100 percent of your personal wealth invested in the auto industry? What about high tech? The same principle applies to "human assets": Why employ just one type of person? Might you be missing out on some of the unique knowledge, skills, abilities, and approaches to problem solving that can be provided by individuals from disparate backgrounds, educations, or locales? Of course you might!

Still Struggling

As a rule, affirmative action is legally required *only* in firms that have, or are bidding for, government contracts. In addition, in some cases where diversity has been neglected, courts of law may impose affirmative action policies as sanctions for unfair hiring practices. However, affirmative action is *not* a substitute for appropriately managing diversity.

Challenges in Managing Employee Diversity

Diversity offers challenges as well as opportunities. Challenges include issues such as feelings of reverse discrimination, the potential for backlash by current employees, and further alienation of underrepresented minority groups by improperly singling them out.

Valuing Employee Diversity

Truly valuing diversity among employees is paramount in diversity management. All too often, employers hire for diversity, but then reward individuals for conformity to organizational norms. It is the responsibility of the HR manager to seek out, listen to, and synthesize sometimes drastically divergent viewpoints among employees and managers with varied backgrounds.

Individual versus Group Fairness

Understanding differences between individual and group fairness is also incredibly important in managing diversity. It is important that managers be in touch with the feelings of the individuals within groups. While management frequently attempts to treat work groups equally, individuals within those groups often do not view their managers' decisions as being individually fair. These individuals might attribute their treatment to characteristics such as race, gender, or ethnicity.

PROBLEM 3-3

While it might not occur to many managers, family status or number of dependents is also a basis of diversity. Many firms struggle with equity issues associated with providing benefits that affect single-parent families, married couples with children, and people with other family structures equally. Keeping this in mind, to what extent should employers be responsible for the appropriate care of their employees' children?

SOLUTION

As values have shifted in this country, employees are becoming more and more concerned with their family life and with issues surrounding the care of their children. Companies may view this as a nonethical question and simply an issue that is necessary in order to attract and retain high-quality employees. However, there is also an ethical question involved: does the company's commitment and responsibility to its employees start and end at the time clock? More and more people are saying that the company's responsibility extends beyond those boundaries. Some would point to the common practice of providing health-care benefits and life insurance as an indication of this expanded view of the company's responsibilities. Certainly companies can expect that they will do better at attracting and retaining the best, and at obtaining better loyalty, commitment, and performance from employees, if they are willing to go the extra mile to ensure that some of the employees' family life issues are covered.

Resistance to Change

People are inherently resistant to change. For example, certain individuals who are used to having a strong influence on decisions may feel threatened by a new member of the company or departmental team. These influential players may now be faced with the need to further discuss and defend their ideas and the merits of those ideas, and they may feel that their value to the organization has been decreased because of this. If employees in your organization have been surrounded by, or worked with, only one type of person for a number of years, it may be difficult for them to change their patterns of interaction to deal with a new, diverse group of employees.

Group Cohesiveness and Interpersonal Conflict

Again, humans inherently gravitate toward people who are similar to themselves (this is called the *theory of homophilic tendencies*); this similarity could be based on race, ethnicity, gender, or something as simple as being fans of the same baseball team or alumni of the same university. Creating consistencies among individuals is important to group cohesiveness. Many times, activities such as team building, light discussion, or outside-of-work interaction can facilitate cohesiveness. Conversely, interpersonal conflict can work to the detriment of managing diversity. Perhaps two individuals have a verbal altercation at work—what is the basis of the disagreement? Is it possible that there is some bias based on race, ethnicity, gender, or other characteristic? While some level of conflict in organizations is *good*, dysfunctional conflict can undermine efforts to create an inclusive workplace.

 **PROBLEM 3-4**

Many organizations have policies requiring that people from certain demographic groups (such as women and African Americans) sit on certain (or all) committees. Are there any dangers to such a policy? Could the potential benefits outweigh the potential costs?

 **SOLUTION**

Yes, there are potential dangers. For example, for the sake of fulfilling the quota, people who would be better contributors to the purpose of the committee may be passed over, while those who are given the posts may be viewed as "token" members and not taken seriously. Additionally, members of majority or nondesignated minority groups may feel discriminated against because of their lessened representation.

The benefits, however, may outweigh the potential costs. Giving minority group members seats on committees may cause the groups that they are members of to feel more represented and empowered as a whole. Also, viewpoints that possibly were not brought forth on such committees may now be heard, potentially increasing the bottom line of the organization.

Segmented Communication Networks

Based on the theory of homophilic tendencies, individuals who are similar to one another might communicate only with their small, personal network of individuals within a firm. This can become problematic when information is not communicated effectively or efficiently throughout the organization because of such segmented networks.

Resentment

Most often, resentment is based on either a lack of information or inaccurate information. For example, misunderstandings about the application of affirmative action policies or the process of conducting an availability analysis might cause existing employees to question hiring practices. As with most management decisions, honesty is the best policy—the free flow of information and transparency in decision making can normally quell these problems.

Backlash

Similarly, sometimes members of the "majority" group feel that they have been the victims of "reverse discrimination" and lash out against new hires or all members of a particular minority group. As with resentment, transparency and honesty by management are effective in combating this problem.

Diversity in Organizations

Although they are not the only aspects of diversity, race, ethnicity, and gender tend to have a major impact on how people relate to and understand one another. In this section, groups that have traditionally been underrepresented in the corporate mainstream are described and discussed. Of course, these group-based descriptions have limitations, as not all persons within these groups are discriminated against. An individual may also belong to several of these groups. While stereotypes can often be harmful, understanding differences between and similarities among groups is an important step in promoting tolerance in the workplace.

African Americans

African Americans currently make up approximately 12 percent of the U.S. workforce. They were struggling for acceptance and equality before the establishment of the Civil Rights Act of 1964, and have continued to do so. While fairly prominent, African Americans are still tremendously underrepresented in the upper levels of management, as well as in politics.

Asian Americans

Sometimes referred to as the "model minority," Asian Americans make up a very small percentage of the U.S. workforce—approximately 5 percent. Asian Americans have markedly higher levels of education and small business ownership than either other minority groups or European Americans.

People with Disabilities

This is perhaps one of the most misunderstood segments of the workforce. It is estimated that up to 30 percent of the U.S. workforce has some type of documented disability. The 1990 Americans with Disabilities Act was established (among other reasons) to protect this group from unreasonable demands and employment discrimination. It should be noted that the ADA applies only to companies with more than 15 employees in order to protect family-run and small businesses.

The Foreign Born

Foreign-born employees range from illegal immigrants to high-level executives who were born outside of the country in which they work and live. Many times, an underlying bias exists in interacting with such individuals, as it may be assumed that they are not citizens, that they are living in the country illegally, or that they have difficulty speaking English. These are simply *not* true assumptions. Foreign-born employees often bring a unique and immeasurably valuable point of view to an organization.

Homosexuals

Homosexuality spans all racial, ethnic, and social classes. It is estimated that 10 percent of the U.S. workforce is homosexual. Terminology and grouping of individuals has been an especially sensitive subject when discussing this group. Many times, all gay, lesbian, bisexual, and transgender people are lumped into the same category—it should be noted that each of these is a unique disposition and that they are not interchangeable. Unfortunately, many states do not protect homosexuals from employment discrimination, but nonetheless, discriminating against an individual for any reason can result in serious economic and public relations consequences.

Latinos (Hispanic Americans)

Hispanics are the largest minority group in the United States, and one of the fastest growing. They are actually the majority population (or close to it) in states such as New Mexico, Florida, and California. A rule of thumb is that there are more Hispanics in the United States than there are Canadians in Canada!

Currently, there are approximately 33 million Hispanics in the United States, making up approximately 12 percent of the U.S. population. It is projected that there will be more than 50 million Hispanics by 2020. According to Census projections, Hispanics will be 25 percent of the total U.S. population by 2050. This group has accounted for 40 percent of the population growth in the United States in the past decade, growing at 60 percent—10 times the rate of non-Hispanics. The U.S. Latino population has grown faster than predicted since 1990 and is now approximately the same size as the African American population.

Younger/Older Workers

Generational conflict is perhaps the last acceptable form of discrimination at work. While older workers are a protected class (if they are over the age of 40), it is perfectly legal to discriminate against a younger worker regardless of that worker's skill set. With the baby boomer generation preparing to retire en masse, a shift in the demography of the workforce is on the horizon.

Women

Women actually make up more than 50 percent of the U.S. population. Since underrepresentation is normally determined by the *power* rather than the *size* of a group, however, women are included in this section. The gender wage gap has been well documented (it is reported that women earn approximately between $0.72 and $0.87 for each dollar earned by men in similar positions), but it should be noted that research has found that minority women are even more severely underpaid and underrepresented in higher-level positions.

Improving the Management of Diversity

Organizations that have made the greatest strides in successfully managing diversity tend to share a number of characteristics. In order to facilitate the management of diversity, it is important to incorporate the following.

Cultivate Top Management Commitment to Valuing Diversity

"Buy-in" from upper-level management is essential to implementing any diversity program. When lower-level employees see the commitment of top-level employees, they, too, are more likely to embrace the tenets of the program. Additionally, when high-level decision makers champion an effort, they are more likely to provide the resources necessary for diversity initiatives to succeed.

Diversity Training Programs

Proactive, well-designed programs based on awareness contribute to the effective management of diversity. We cannot expect people to innately or naturally understand how to manage diversity effectively. While it is the "right thing to do" and a cost-effective approach to improving corporate performance, the proper instruction of employees in how to implement this approach is crucial for its success.

Support Groups

Often, minority employees feel marginalized. The creation of employee networks or support groups based on certain characteristics generally helps these employees feel important and valued.

Accommodation of Family Needs

Family structure, an often-overlooked aspect of diversity, can lead to enormous stress. Employee benefits such as on-site or reduced-cost day care and offering alternative work schedules or telecommuting options can aid in retention of employees and create greater productivity overall.

Senior Mentoring Programs

Research continues to validate the idea that one of the most effective ways to empower and retain employees of all backgrounds is through the creation and implementation of mentoring programs. One-on-one relationships between senior and more junior employees create lasting relationships on both the professional and interpersonal levels.

Diversity Audits

A diversity audit is sometimes performed to check up on the firm's current mix of employees. Performing diversity audits proactively (rather than in response to some complaint or as a sanction) can help to ensure that the firm's practices further promote the equal treatment of all employees and applicants.

Management Responsibility and Accountability

As with any task, assigning responsibility and accountability to particular managers is incredibly important. When many individuals in the organization are responsible for making sure that the organization honors its commitment to diversity, the likelihood of compliance increases tremendously.

Two potential pitfalls must be avoided if diversity management programs are to be successful. These pitfalls are the appearance of "white male bashing" and the promotion of stereotypes. At the very least, management should continually emphasize the positive aspects of capitalizing on employee diversity by framing it as something that is in the best interests of all employees to enable the firm to gain a competitive advantage in the marketplace. Also, managers must realize that they cannot draw conclusions about a particular person based simply on his or her group characteristics. Differences between individuals within a given group are almost always greater than the typical differences between two groups.

 PROBLEM 3-5

Many managers and executives use golf outings as an opportunity to combine business and pleasure. How could this practice damage an organization's diversity efforts? Are there any recreational activities that could enhance diversity efforts?

 SOLUTION

While many more women and members of minority groups are golfing today than ever before, the sport has traditionally been one favored by white males. In fact, women and minority-group members still golf less than white males. This means that there is a potential for an "old boys club" to develop around the sport, creating an adverse impact on women and minority-group members. Those who play the game with their managers may be seen as being on the "inside track" and receiving greater recognition, promotions, or other benefits than those who do not. This situation creates a very real danger in many organizations today.

Recreational activities that could enhance diversity efforts would include activities that people of various races, ethnicities, sexes, and so on enjoy and can compete in equally. Basketball, softball, or other athletic activities may work, as may less physical activities, such as playing card games. Athletic activities could, and should, also incorporate "mixed leagues" so that both men and women can participate.

Chapter Summary

Proper implementation and management of diversity is the cornerstone of low-cost, high-impact HR-related changes that can be implemented in an organization. Simply by providing proper training, education, and inspiration to the employees of their firm, HR professionals can improve the functioning and efficiency of their organization. While many people argue that linking diversity practices to bottom-line figures is problematic, those firms that have combined unique talents, ideas, and problem-solving skills effectively will attest to the improved efficiency of their organizations.

QUIZ

1. **Which minority group is often referred to as the "model minority"?**
   A. African Americans
   B. Asian Americans
   C. Hispanic Americans
   D. Arab Americans

2. **The Americans with Disabilities Act applies to organizations with more than this number of employees:**
   A. 5
   B. 10
   C. 15
   D. 20

3. **What group is the largest minority group in the United States?**
   A. Hispanic Americans
   B. African Americans
   C. Asian Americans
   D. Arab Americans

4. **Which of the following is not an issue for women in the workplace?**
   A. Gender wage gap
   B. Disproportionate percentage of the population
   C. Lower levels of power in organizations
   D. Tensions of gender identity

5. **What form of discrimination is legally acceptable in the workplace?**
   A. Racial discrimination
   B. Sexual orientation discrimination
   C. Generational discrimination
   D. Gender discrimination

6. **The theory of homophilic tendencies refers to**
   A. The human tendency to inherently gravitate toward people who are similar to ourselves.
   B. Romantic or sexual attraction toward or behavior among members of the same sex.
   C. The tendency of individuals to associate and bond with their opposites.
   D. The issues that arise when organizations are oversaturated with one minority group.

7. **All but which of the following are part of today's conception of the management of diversity?**
    A. Educational background
    B. Functional area
    C. Communication style
    D. Affirmative action placement goals

8. **When addressing diversity from a strategic sense, managers should**
    A. Determine areas of deficiency in their organizations.
    B. Determine what sorts of employees might bring unique perspectives to the organization.
    C. Know the differences between affirmative action policy and diversity management.
    D. Do all of the above.

9. **Discrimination against members of a dominant or majority group is referred to as**
    A. Ableism.
    B. Egalitarianism.
    C. Reverse discrimination.
    D. Anglo-Saxon discrimination.

10. **What piece of legislation was passed specifically to enforce the acceptance and equality of African Americans?**
    A. Fair Labor Standards Act of 1938
    B. Civil Rights Act of 1964
    C. Jim Crow laws
    D. Equal Rights Amendment of 1972

Part II

Hiring for Needs

chapter **4**

Job Analysis

This chapter covers job analysis—the first stage of the hiring process. When most people think of human resource management, or its previous incarnation as "staffing" or "personnel," they typically think about the process of hiring employees. The first two phases in this hiring process are job analysis and recruiting.

CHAPTER OBJECTIVES

After completing this chapter, the student should be able to

1. Describe various forms of organization design.
2. Understand the options available for conducting a job analysis.
3. Understand the importance of job descriptions and how to write one that is well formed.
4. Understand the options available for staffing your organization.

Strategy and Organizational Structure

An organization develops a business strategy by establishing a set of long-term goals. The business strategy that management selects determines the structure, or restructuring, that is most appropriate. Moreover, management selects HR strategies to fit and support its overall business strategies and organizational structure.

 PROBLEM 4-1

Implicit in this chapter is the view that organizational change is necessary for a firm's survival. However, organizational change often places individual employees under considerable stress, particularly resulting from constantly having to learn new skills and job requirements. Is the organization ethically responsible for protecting employees from these stressful changes?

 SOLUTION

While there may be differing views on this subject, let us suggest an answer that seems most reasonable. When job losses occur because of organizational change or economic downturn, it seems reasonable that the organization has an ethical responsibility to provide its employees with *assistance* in handling and dealing with the resulting stress. Successful programs include outplacement services, severance packages to assist the employees during the transitional period, and counseling services. It is probably unreasonable to expect any organization to *protect* individuals from the stresses of life. However, it may also be reasonable to assume that the organization may have a stronger ethical responsibility to long-term employees who may be nearing retirement.

Designing the Organization

Most organizations fit into one of three categories: (1) bureaucratic, (2) flat, or (3) boundaryless.

Bureaucratic organizations consist of hierarchies with many levels of management and are driven by a top-down, or command-and-control, approach in which managers provide considerable direction and have fairly direct control over those reporting to them (the classic example of an institution utilizing this approach is the military). The bureaucratic organization is based on a functional division of labor, where employees are divided into groups based on their positions and duties. Work specialization is another feature of this type of organization, as employees spend most of their time working individually or at a specific task.

Flat organizations have only a few levels of managers and emphasize a decentralized approach to management, encouraging high employee involvement in business decisions. The purpose of this structure is to create independent small businesses or enterprises that can respond rapidly to customers' needs or changes in the business environment. Flat organizations are useful for companies that are implementing a Total Quality Management (TQM) strategy, a concept developed and coined by W. Edwards Deming that encompasses all aspects of the product delivery process, including streamlining, production, and improving customer service. TQM strategy is a precursor to more modern approaches such as Six Sigma and ISO 9000/9001.

Boundaryless organizations enable companies to form relationships (joint ventures, intellectual property agreements, marketing distribution channels, or financial resources pooling) with customers, suppliers, and/or competitors. Companies often use a boundaryless organizational structure when they (1) collaborate with customers or suppliers to provide better-quality products or services, (2) are entering foreign markets that have barriers to entry for foreign competitors, or (3) need to manage the risk of developing an expensive new technology. Boundaryless organizations share many of the characteristics of flat organizations and have a strong emphasis on teams, which are likely to include employees representing different companies in a joint venture.

Once the format of the organization has been established, it is important to determine how the organization's "work flow" is arranged. Work-flow analysis studies how work moves from the customer through the organization, to the point at which the work leaves the organization as a product or service for the customer. Work-flow analysis often reveals that some steps or jobs can be combined, simplified, or even eliminated. The information gained also helps determine what is the actual "work" that is done by each person or in each job and how many customers are served by these actions. Through this analysis, jobs that can be eliminated or combined to improve company performance are identified. It is also possible to calculate the number of employees that are necessary to serve the organization's customers as sales climb.

A work-flow analysis is followed by job design and, next, the communication of job expectations to job incumbents. The basis of this process is a job analysis, which requires systematic data gathering and organization of information regarding the tasks and responsibilities of a particular job. Job analysis is useful for recruitment, selection, performance appraisal, compensation, training, and career development activities.

Still Struggling

Organizational design is normally something that is inherited, not set up. While this is sometimes frustrating, most times the design of an organization is organic and develops over many years. If your organization finds it necessary to reorganize, know that it will be a long process that may not be successful if the new design is drastically different from the old one.

Designing Jobs and Conducting a Job Analysis

All the theories of employee motivation suggest that jobs can be designed in ways that improve performance. There are three important influences on job design: (1) work-flow analysis (described earlier), (2) business strategy, and (3) organizational structure based on business strategy.

The first step in a job analysis is to determine who will conduct it. Will this analysis be performed by someone inside the organization? Or will an external group be hired to conduct the analysis? It is important to note that there are ramifications of each choice. Internal analysis may lead to more tailored results, based on specific knowledge of the organization, but it could also result in an overly politicized version of the truth that may be influenced by lingering bias and personal feelings about particular employees. On the other hand, external analysis may prove costly and may be perceived as wasteful. In any event, whoever performs it, job analysis must be presented to employees as a tool for improving processes and growing the organization—not as a method of eliminating staff.

Next, the method of job analysis must be determined. Some popular methods are briefly described here.

- *Task inventory analysis.* A task inventory (or list of activities performed by the employees in an organization) is created, and each employee's tasks are determined, either via interviews (preferable) or via surveys.

- *Critical incident technique.* This technique focuses on individual employees (usually in an interview setting) describing what happens when specific incidents occur (e.g., an unusually boisterous customer comes into the store demanding a refund). These behavioral interviews can focus on regularly occurring tasks or extraordinary sets of circumstances.

- *Position analysis questionnaire (PAQ).* The PAQ is a structured job analysis questionnaire that measures job characteristics and relates them to human characteristics rather than describing the specific tasks or duties required. In fact, PAQs are very popular, and many consulting firms offer this service via the Internet or through paper-and-pencil questionnaires.

- *Functional job analysis.* Developed by the U.S. Department of Labor, this is a quantitative method of job analysis that involves an inventory of functions and work activities falling into three broad worker function categories: data, people, and things.

Regardless of the method of job analysis selected, it is important to remember that no single method is perfect. While working in HR, you may find that each organization has its own unique approach to job analysis.

Another consideration in performing job analysis is the set of legal ramifications associated with conducting it. Job analysis is generally performed to match an individual's job description to the tasks that the individual actually performs on a day-to-day basis (you would be shocked at how different official written job descriptions can be from the actual work done) and can also aid in legal defensibility. For example, employers can avoid wrongful termination lawsuits by tailoring employees' job descriptions to the jobs they actually perform. Suppose you hire a recent college graduate as an information technology specialist, you are unhappy with the employee's performance, and you terminate the employee for updating the company's Web site incorrectly. If the individual's job description does not include Web site development and the skills required do not include Web site design and HTML programming, this individual would have a compelling lawsuit against your organization.

PROBLEM 4-2

Obtain copies of job descriptions for clerical positions at the firm where you work. What types of information do they contain? Do they give you enough information to explain what the job involves and how to do it? How would you improve on the descriptions?

SOLUTION

Based on our experience, it is very likely that at least some of the job descriptions will not contain all the information that is supposed to be there. Use this as an opportunity to discuss with a manager the problems that may be created by the missing information.

In the end, it is of the utmost importance to understand that no inventory of job functions can be substituted for a knowledgeable manager who knows how and when job-related tasks can be accomplished. For this reason, including the manager who will have day-to-day interaction with the newly hired employees is important when determining the scope and description of a particular job.

 Still Struggling

No one method of job analysis is perfect. In fact, it is likely that some hybrid form will arise once the parameters have been determined. Don't feel that your analysis needs to be 100 percent identical to one of the methods discussed here.

Job Descriptions

A job description is a portrait of a job. It may be specific (a detailed summary) or general (associated with work-flow strategies that emphasize innovation, flexibility, and loose work planning). In any event, it is a written document that identifies, defines, and describes a job in terms of its duties, responsibilities, working conditions, and specifications. A proper job description accurately portrays the work done in a particular position and should contain a job summary (the overall goal or purpose of the job), job duties and responsibilities (what is specifically required to be done), and job specifications and minimum qualifications (the characteristics of the individual in that position).

Special Cases

As we all know, the workforce is rapidly changing, as are the skills, knowledge, abilities, and opportunities associated with individuals entering and leaving the workforce. That being said, it is important to note two new and useful tools in staffing one's organization.

Contingent Workers

There are two types of workers: contingent (those having a tentative relationship with an employer) and core (those having full-time jobs with an employer). Firms hire contingent workers to help them deal with temporary increases in their workload (like a temporary employee, or "temp") or to do work that is not part of the organization's core set of capabilities (as in the case of hiring a specialized consultant). Additional types of contingent workers could include outsourced or subcontracted workers, contract workers, and college interns who are hired for specific tasks or to reduce costs associated with the firm's primary business.

Outsourcing has increasingly become the wave of the future, with more and more companies looking to the "virtual corporation" as an organizational model. Consistent with this trend, human resource activities such as payroll, benefits, training, recruiting, and performance evaluation are being outsourced by organizations as well. There are both advantages and disadvantages to outsourcing these activities, and the costs and benefits should be considered before making a decision to outsource or retain a specific job function, role, or task. For example, while there are benefit costs associated with the employment of most contingent workers, these workers may also be able or willing to leave an organization quickly. Additionally, given the lack of security and fringe benefits, contingent workers might demand higher hourly wages to offset these perceived inconveniences. Temporary or seasonal workers and interns also are likely to be in search of permanent employment elsewhere, thus limiting their commitment to an organization where they have been hired as contingent employees.

 **PROBLEM 4-3**

Why is it so difficult to predict whether a new employee will be a highly motivated employee? What factors can influence employee motivation?

SOLUTION

It is difficult to predict an employee's motivation because motivation is a complex concept and has numerous sources, including the employee's needs and abilities, the characteristics of the job, the extent to which the employee values growth, the employee's goals, the characteristics of the organization, and the way the job is designed. Factors influencing employee motivation are revealed through various motivation theories, including the two-factor theory (consisting of a hygiene factor that removes dissatisfaction and another motivational factor), goal setting, and job characteristics theory (a complex theory that, at its core, focuses on tailoring specific job characteristics or duties to motivate employees). Such theories suggest that jobs can be designed to increase motivation and performance.

Flexible Work Schedules

Flexible work schedules alter the typical job schedule while keeping the job design and the employee-employer relationship intact. Common types of these schedules include flexible hours (e.g., allowing an employee to choose when he or she performs the standard 8 work hours during the day), condensed or compressed workweeks (e.g., working four 10-hour days instead of five 8-hour days), and telecommuting (using technology to work from home or elsewhere to complete regular tasks). Today, flexibility and freedom are more valued by workers. Therefore, employers can use inexpensive (or in many cases no-expense) tactics like this one to improve employee satisfaction and decrease burnout.

 PROBLEM 4-4

Many employees and union representatives complain bitterly about the practice of outsourcing work, particularly to foreign countries. Part of the complaint is that companies institute such practices to avoid paying fair wages and providing the employee benefits that U.S. workers expect. Is this an ethical issue?

 SOLUTION

Yes, this is an ethical issue. Anytime you have a situation that pits financial considerations against questions of fair and appropriate treatment of people, you have an ethical question. As with most ethical dilemmas, there is not an easy answer to this one. On the one hand, you have the financial

well-being of the company that is facing worldwide competition, and on the other hand, you have the ability of workers to earn a decent wage and to gain reasonable benefits. If a company unilaterally decides to forgo outsourcing of this kind but then is forced out of business because of its competition's lower costs, has an ethical decision been made? Some would say yes; others would say no. Certainly, in a case where a company is highly profitable and is not in danger of losing market share because of its costs, outsourcing of this kind could easily be seen as unethical. Additionally, loss of U.S. jobs has a negative impact on the economy, a topic that has received a great deal of attention in recent years. Most situations are not this clear-cut, but this one does help exhibit the difficulties that company executives face in making these decisions.

Chapter Summary

Conducting a proper job analysis can help improve the efficiency of an organization in many ways. Creating well-written, accurate job descriptions can lead to increased worker effectiveness, lower levels of monotony and boredom, and efficient use of employees' talents and interests, as well as eliminate claims of unfair dismissal. But the value of job analysis does not end here; when an organization fully understands the knowledge, skills, and abilities necessary for each position in the organization, it can effectively hire, create new positions, alter existing positions, and even eliminate certain existing positions. Understanding the needs of the firm's workers and its positions can only lead to an organization's operating more effectively.

QUIZ

1. **Which of the following is not a type of contingent worker?**
   A. College interns
   B. Temporary employees
   C. Full-time employees
   D. Contract workers

2. **Which of the following is not one of the most common types of flexible work schedules?**
   A. Flexible work hours
   B. Condensed/compressed workweeks
   C. Telecommuting
   D. Core workweeks

3. **Which of the following is not one of the four key elements of a job description?**
   A. Job summary
   B. Preferred qualifications
   C. Identification information
   D. Job specifications and minimum qualifications

4. **Job characteristics theory can be defined as**
   A. A theory that states that employee motivation depends on job characteristics such as skill variety, task identity, task significance, autonomy, and feedback.
   B. A theory that states that motivation and job satisfaction depend on the fit between the employee's abilities or needs and the job and organizational characteristics.
   C. A concept that talks about how to design a job so that it is simple for an employee.
   D. A concept that states that an employee will adapt to the job characteristics that he or she needs to, while eliminating unnecessary work.

5. **Former General Electric chairman Jack Welch wanted to eliminate vertical and horizontal boundaries within the company and break down external barriers between the company and its customers and suppliers. What kind of organization design does this describe?**
   A. Bureaucratic organization
   B. Flat organization
   C. Boundaryless organization
   D. Centralized organization

6. Total Quality Management can be defined as
   A. Using work-flow analysis to organize around tasks, not outcomes.
   B. Using work-flow analysis to identify a company's core processes involved in producing its product or delivering its service to the customer, and organizing its HR around those core processes to improve organizational performance.
   C. Using basic principles of engineering focusing on integrating work to process information.
   D. Using basic principles of engineering focusing on activities in the work flow instead of just integrating results.

7. Self-managed teams share all but which of the following skills?
   A. Interpersonal skills
   B. Administrative skills
   C. Technical skills
   D. Group-thinking skills

8. Which of the following is not a typical organizational format?
   A. Boundaryless
   B. Flat
   C. Hierarchical
   D. Line and staff

9. A team that consists of members who are located in different locations around the globe and work together using technology to communicate is called a:
   A. Problem-solving team.
   B. Special-purpose team.
   C. Virtual team.
   D. Self-managed team.

10. Company A is referred to as top-heavy and hierarchical. What type of organizational structure best defines this company?
    A. Bureaucratic organization
    B. Flat organization
    C. Boundaryless organization
    D. Centralized organization

chapter **5**

Employee Selection

This chapter discusses the process for, and importance of, selecting employees. Human resource planning is the overall process that an organization uses to ensure that it has the right amount, and the right kinds, of people to deliver a particular level of output or services in the future. Failures in HR planning can lead to labor shortages, layoffs, and significant financial costs. For this reason, job analysis (discussed in the previous chapter) is of key importance in planning for the future of your organization's labor force. By understanding what each individual in the organization actually *does* on a day-to-day basis, you can properly represent your organization during the recruiting process.

CHAPTER OBJECTIVES

After completing this chapter, the student should be able to

1. Understand the importance of forecasting employee need.
2. Describe the hiring process and its iterative nature.
3. Identify issues in recruiting and selection.
4. Understand the importance and impact of antidiscrimination legislation in the hiring process.

Forecasting Needs for Employees

The first step in establishing a recruiting plan is using the knowledge gained in the job analysis process to determine, or forecast, the number and types of employees your organization will need to meet the expected level of future performance. Several quantitative techniques exist for determining levels of demand, including regression analysis (a statistical method using past data to determine projected future need) and ratio analysis (creating a ratio of employee input to product or service output to try to determine how many additional employees are needed for a new level of output). Additionally, judgmental methods such as "top-down" (using national- or international-level information to determine the needs of specific branches) or "bottom-up" (using information from individual locations to determine companywide needs) analysis are valuable approaches to determining employee demand.

While calculating demand for employees based on the organization's needs is certainly important, many organizations neglect to determine the *supply* available in the local worker pool. Determining the number of qualified and interested potential employees in your labor pool is at least as important as determining your firm's demand for employees, if not more important. Complex techniques such as Markov analysis (in which a sequence of events is analyzed to determine the capacity, reliability, and availability of a particular skill or skill set) or simpler, more judgmental techniques like succession planning (determining which in-house employees will be developed to assume a higher-level position in the future) can be used to determine the amount of qualified labor in your predetermined population.

Whether you are using a complex or an anecdotal technique, identifying the number of qualified applicants can help determine the goal, breadth, and target media market for a job posting. For example, if an accounting firm is located in a large, metropolitan city with a fairly well educated population, the HR department might be able to recruit only locally and spare the expense of recruiting travel. Conversely, a similarly sized accounting firm operating in a lower-income and less educated area with few institutions of higher education nearby might need to cast a wider net and seek applicants from a larger radius.

 **PROBLEM 5-1**

Develop a forecast of occupational market conditions for various jobs, such as accountant, nurse, and engineer, for the next five years.

 **SOLUTION**

The forecast should include projected growth in the number of these jobs, number of program graduates, and salary growth. Projected retirements and current economic conditions should also be taken into account. Visit online the Department of Labor, salary.com, and other Internet resources to collect this information.

The Hiring Process

The hiring process does not stop when a new employee fills out the appropriate paperwork and reports for his or her first day on the job. The entire hiring process actually has three components:

1. *Recruiting* entails marketing the job and the company in which it resides. This process is used to establish a pool of qualified and interested applicants from as diverse backgrounds as possible.

2. *Selection* is the process of choosing the most qualified candidate from this pool of applicants to fill the position. This candidate will be picked based on a number of criteria, including, but not limited to, previous experience, strong references, specific knowledge or trades, and fit with the company as a whole.

3. *Socialization* is the process by which the selected applicant learns the "ins and outs" of his or her specific day-to-day job, becomes adjusted to the company culture, and is assisted throughout the process of coming onboard.

Choosing the right person for a job can make a tremendous difference in productivity and customer satisfaction. Choosing the wrong person can result in sluggish operations and lost business and customers. For these reasons, it is important that each step of the staffing process be managed carefully.

Unfortunately, all too often, emphasis is placed on selection, and recruiting and socialization are neglected. Recruiting, when correctly done, can make the selection process easier and, in general, much more pleasant. Socialization is a useful tool to help qualified applicants succeed in their new positions, limit attrition tremendously, and improve the overall culture of the organization dramatically.

Despite the obvious importance of selecting the best people from the available talent, the hiring process is replete with challenges. The most difficult of these are determining what characteristics are of greatest importance to performance (and then measuring those characteristics), evaluating applicants' motivation levels, and deciding who should make the selection decision.

When developing a plan for hiring, it is important to base the criteria on elements of the job description, beginning with the minimum requirements. In addition to these requirements, a list of the characteristics that are most important for high levels of performance must be created.

Once this list of criteria has been established, measurement of these characteristics must also be agreed upon: How do we measure conscientiousness? How can we assess an individual's level of motivation? How can we test an individual's content knowledge?

Creating and discussing consistency in measurement can alleviate problems further down the road within the group or department that has been given the task of hiring the new employee. The best effort to standardize these measures will still, no doubt, result in a fair amount of variance in results and evaluation, but it should give a clearer picture of the best candidates for the job—in most cases, the old adage "the cream rises to the top" rings true in the hiring situation.

Ultimately, some call—whom to hire or even not to hire—must be made. Most organizations will charge a group of individuals with coming to a collaborative decision in selecting a new employee. Sometimes, however, the human resources department will go through the entire hiring process with little or no input from the person or people who will ultimately be managing this employee. Other firms allow the direct supervisor to make a final hiring decision after initial screening by others or by the HR department. Whatever the decision of the organization, it is imperative that the person who is *ultimately* responsible for having the last word in hiring be determined and agreed upon before the selection process begins.

PROBLEM 5-2

Suppose you are asked to write a recommendation letter for a friend whom you like, but whom you consider unreliable. Would it be ethical for you to write a positive reference even though you anticipate that your friend will not be a good employee? If not, would it be ethical for you to agree to write the letter although you know that you will not be very positive in your assessment of your friend's abilities?

**SOLUTION**

While it can be uncomfortable to refuse to write a recommendation or to tell a person that you will not write a very positive recommendation, either response would be an ethical one. Giving information that is not true or misleading someone about what kind of letter you plan to write is unethical and dishonest, and is normally done in an effort to make life easier for yourself. Ethical actions are often uncomfortable and can be incredibly difficult, but they are important in maintaining your own personal character standards.

Issues in Recruiting

When embarking on the hiring process, addressing several issues that can, and normally will, arise in the recruiting process is of the utmost importance. The following are situations to be aware of and questions that the firm should consider during recruiting.

Nontraditional Recruiting in the Current Labor Market

Whom will your organization seek to recruit? In the twenty-first century, there are a myriad of options for employees and employers with regard to the labor market. Contingent workers (discussed in the previous chapter) may be an option for your firm, and such positions may be desirable to certain members of the workforce. A number of retired workers are also now seeking new employment—would your firm consider hiring them? There are also many potential employees who are seeking greater freedom and flexibility in their work schedule. Is your firm prepared to offer such flexibility in order to attract different groups of job seekers?

External versus Internal Candidates

When you are recruiting, it is imperative that you consider whom you would like to include in your labor pool. Depending on the size of the organization and the experience of its employees, firms may decide to concentrate on internal candidates as opposed to external candidates. However, if no current workers are qualified to fill a vacant position, candidates from outside the company must be considered. There are obviously costs associated with looking outside the organization, and not necessarily only economic ones. For example, how might current employees react to an "outsider"? Does an external hire send a message to the remaining employees that they are not valued or qualified for higher-level positions?

 PROBLEM 5-3

Seek out several classified and display ads from a Sunday paper's help wanted ads or from any online job board. Analyze the effectiveness of these ads using the guidelines discussed in this chapter.

 SOLUTION

The effectiveness should be analyzed using the following list: attracts attention, develops interest, creates desire, and prompts action.

Recruiting Protected Classes

It is imperative that you be familiar with your company's policies on hiring and recruiting members of minority groups or protected classes and that you fully understand any related federal or state laws regarding diversity in the workplace (detailed in Chapter 3). Start by conducting an availability analysis to determine the demographic makeup of the labor pool. Next, make sure that your organization is in agreement with regard to what segments of the population the firm is trying to reach and how your business profile matches the constituency you seek to serve.

Planning the Recruitment Effort and Job Search

First, your organization must confirm that a search for a new employee is necessary by simply weighing its options and asking, "Must we hire?" If the answer is yes, then it is time to consider potential conflicts that may arise. For example, what if there are no good matches internally or externally? Or, what level of flexibility in compensation is available? Next, during the planning stages of recruitment, solidify where you plan to recruit, what kind of candidate you need to fill the opening, and how many positions this opening creates. Once all of this basic information is established, the recruiting process should go much more smoothly.

Still Struggling

Most people fear a failed search; however, "no hire" is still, actually, a successful search. Sometimes the pool of applicants just does not yield any qualified candidates. While leaving a position vacant can result in decreased outcomes, hiring an ill-prepared applicant could be even more costly.

Issues in Employee Selection

Some of the most contentious decisions made in organizations center on selection issues. The main issues to consider are applicants' responses to selection tools and managers' input on the selection tools and process.

Reliability and Validity of the Selection Process

It is of the utmost importance that the selection process be both reliable and valid. *Reliability* of the selection process means that if it were conducted by someone else or at a different time, the same decision would be made. *Validity* of the selection process means that the criteria, tools, and information utilized to make the selection are appropriate. Ask yourself if the process is flawed. Then consider whether or not the outcome would be the same if the process were repeated.

Selection Tools

All stakeholders should participate in determining what tools will be used to evaluate applicants. No matter what tools are selected, it is important that the type and scope of each of the following components be clearly communicated to the applicant:

- *Letters of recommendation.* How many are needed, and whom should they come from? Since recommendations are almost always positive, what are you, as the hiring party, looking for in these letters?
- *Application forms.* What relevant and legal information will be collected from the applicants?

- *Ability tests.* What kinds of ability tests are necessary in determining an applicant's fit with the job? Will you be able to match this information with the job analysis results?

- *Personality tests.* Personality-based hiring has become increasingly popular since the late 1990s. What sort of information are you seeking to receive from these tests? What personality characteristics match what jobs in your organization?

- *Psychological tests.* Are such tests necessary? What information from a psychological test would it be appropriate to analyze?

- *Interviews.* Who will be present during the interview? Will the same questions be asked of each interviewee? How will behavioral questions be asked? How will the quality of answers be evaluated?

- *Drug tests.* What is the legality of drug tests? What are the costs and benefits of performing such tests? Is a drug test a necessary item for safety or job requirements within your organization?

- *Reference checks.* As with letters of recommendation, make sure to confirm what you are looking for and what questions to ask to obtain such information. What happens if conflicting information is received from different sources?

- *Background checks.* What are the costs and benefits of these checks? How do you handle the situation if something questionable comes up?

PROBLEM 5-4

Some experts contend that urinalysis is an invasion of privacy and therefore should be prohibited unless there is reasonable cause to suspect an employee of drug use. Is it ethical for companies to insist that applicants undergo urinalysis? Suppose, on the other hand, a company that wants to save on health insurance decides to test the cholesterol levels of all job applicants to eliminate those who are susceptible to heart attacks. Would this practice be ethical? Would it be legal?

 SOLUTION

There are certainly those who consider drug testing an invasion of privacy and argue that drug use off the job should have no bearing on an individual's work performance. Others, however, would argue that our society has identified drug use as a serious problem that has high costs to individuals and to society as a whole; therefore, companies have an ethical responsibility to help solve that problem. Cholesterol testing, however, delves into a different area. Exclusion of individuals based on high cholesterol levels, whether they are the result of a genetic predisposition or something else, would be considered unethical by most people. Furthermore, legal ramifications are likely, since discrimination against someone because of his or her cholesterol level would probably be considered illegal under the Americans with Disabilities Act (ADA).

Selection and Organization Fit

Since "fit" often cannot be measured by any instrument, how do you evaluate who is the right "fit" for your organization? This is best determined by one-on-one interaction. However, even the most in-depth interaction may not reveal the potential differences between the way an applicant acts during an interview and the way he or she will act as a new employee once he or she is hired. In this case, instincts are usually the best tools the HR manager can use in order to come to a decision. Sometimes the decision will prove to be a good one; at other times, it may be a bad one. In the end, it is important to do as much due diligence as possible to collect information about the applicant before the official hiring.

PROBLEM 5-5

Prepare and give a short presentation titled, "How to Be Effective as an Interviewer."

SOLUTION

There are several things you can do to prepare to be an effective interviewer. Some of the basic ones include structuring the interview, preparing for the interview, establishing rapport, asking questions, closing the interview, and reviewing the interview.

Legal Issues to Consider

Legal concerns can play an exceptionally important role in staffing, particularly in selection. Selection is affected by a number of legal constraints, most notably federal legislation and its definition of illegal discrimination. Negligent hiring concerns have also increased in recent years, and greater attention has been given to this issue. Among the many important policies, laws, and considerations that firms must recognize are the following.

PROBLEM 5-6

Write a short essay discussing some of the ethical and legal considerations in testing.

SOLUTION

State and federal laws, Equal Employment Opportunity Commission (EEOC) guidelines, and court decisions require that you be able to prove that your tests are related to success or failure on the job and that they are not having an adverse impact on members of a protected group. Test takers also have certain basic rights to privacy and information, and the right to expect that the test is equally fair to all.

Discrimination Laws

To lower the chances of lawsuits, firms should ensure that selection techniques are job-related. In other words, the best defense against litigation is evidence of the validity of the selection process. Among the legislation that should be reviewed is the Americans with Disabilities Act of 1990 and the Civil Rights Act of 1964 [see Chapter 2, "Equal Employment Opportunity (EEO) and the Law"].

Affirmative Action

The goal of an affirmative action program is to correct injustices of the past. Federal Executive Order 11246 requires organizations that are government contractors or subcontractors to have affirmative action plans in place. As noted in Chapter 2, "Equal Employment Opportunity (EEO) and the Law," affirmative action is a *policy*—not an actual law.

PROBLEM 5-7

Find at least five employment ads either on the Internet or in a local newspaper that suggest that the company is family-friendly and should appeal to women, minorities, older workers, and single parents. Discuss what the company is doing to be family-friendly.

SOLUTION

Identify statements in the ad that would suggest that the company is aim-ing to be family-friendly. Additionally, evaluate how these policies might affect employees without children. Consider how this approach will affect employees, consumers, and competitors.

Negligent Hiring

Negligent hiring refers to a situation in which an employer fails to use reason-able care in hiring an employee, and that employee then commits a crime while in his or her new position in the organization. In these cases, not only is the individual held accountable for these unlawful actions, but the organization can also be liable for any damage done.

Recruiting and hiring of qualified, committed, and ethical employees is per-haps one of the most important human resource functions. At the end of the day, the "people make the place," and hiring an employee who is a poor fit, is unable to perform the necessary job functions, or is reckless in his or her work can have a catastrophic impact on the firm. Conversely, well-socialized, com-mitted, and productive employees can be key contributors to continued pros-perity and provide an organization with countless opportunities.

 Still Struggling

Legal issues in hiring are incredibly important and much too detailed to cover in the required depth in this chapter. Please use the available resources and consult employment lawyers should any questions arise in the hiring process.

Chapter Summary

While all functions of HR are incredibly valuable, employee selection is perhaps the single most important task completed in the world of human resources. The hire/no hire decision can, in many cases, be a defining moment for an organiza-tion. As discussed earlier in this text, the people make the place, and thus choos-ing whom to hire gives an organization its values, beliefs, ideals, and direction.

Many times the person that you see "on paper" is drastically different from the person who shows up for work on day one. Determining how someone will fit and function within your organization can be the key factor in determining the organization's effectiveness and efficiency.

QUIZ

1. **The hiring process includes all but which of the following components?**
   A. Recruitment
   B. Selection
   C. Orientation
   D. Socialization

2. **The hiring process is fraught with all but which of the following challenges?**
   A. Determining the characteristics that are most important to performance
   B. Writing compliant screening questions
   C. Evaluating applicants' motivation levels
   D. Deciding who should make the selection decision

3. **Executive Order 11246 requires**
   A. Federal contractors to have an affirmative action plan in place.
   B. Minority candidates to be hired when at all possible.
   C. Federal contractors to provide the necessary training and development to bring minority candidates "up to speed."
   D. Federal contractors to ignore gender, race, and sexual orientation when making hiring decisions.

4. **A situation in which an employer fails to use reasonable care in hiring an employee and that employee then commits a crime while in his or her position in the organization is called**
   A. Due diligence.
   B. Liability.
   C. Negligent hiring.
   D. Criminal negligence.

5. **What is the proper sequence of the hiring process?**
   A. Socialization, selection, recruiting
   B. Recruiting, selection, socialization
   C. Recruiting, socialization, selection
   D. Socialization, recruiting, selection

6. **Which of the following positions is likely to require a preemployment background check?**
   A. Recycling technician
   B. Administrative assistant
   C. Mechanic
   D. Morphology technician

7. **Which of the following is not one of the major types of employment tests?**
   A. Intelligence test
   B. Personality test
   C. Writing sample
   D. Simulation

8. **Which of the following are direct costs of making the wrong hiring decision?**
   A. Cost of advertising
   B. Hours spent doing the hiring search
   C. Training expenses
   D. All of the above

9. **Which of the following is *not* a selection tool used by HR personnel?**
   A. In-home observation
   B. Psychological tests
   C. Applications
   D. Interviews

10. **Which of the following groups is affected by job dissatisfaction?**
    A. Managers
    B. Customers
    C. Employees
    D. All of the above

Part III

They're Hired—
Now What?

chapter **6**

Compensation

This chapter covers the concept of compensation. While sometimes puzzling, designing compensation systems is key to maintaining a high-performing workforce. While creating these plans is truly an art, this chapter will give you the basics on how and why certain components are important or essential to employees in your organization.

CHAPTER OBJECTIVES

After completing this chapter, the student should be able to

1. Understand the three components of an employee's total compensation.
2. Determine the key components to consider when designing a compensation system.
3. Understand the key components of job evaluation.
4. Understand the legal constraints on compensation.

Compensation

Compensation is a systematic approach to providing monetary value to employees in exchange for work performed. It is used to hire and keep employees who perform well, and it is a positive way for companies to not only reward employees, but also increase their general happiness. Organizations are able to maintain valued employees by offering them monetary rewards, especially when employees have shown exceptional performance. Compensation in the form of a salary is imperative when a company is competing to attract qualified applicants in the market.

An employee's total compensation has three components. The first and largest element is base compensation (i.e., salary). The second component of total compensation is incentive pay (i.e., bonuses and profit sharing). The third component is benefits or indirect compensation (i.e., insurance, vacation, unemployment, and perks).

PROBLEM 6-1

Some people argue that it is wrong for CEOs to earn multimillion-dollar salaries while some of their employees are earning the minimum wage or even being laid off. Some suggest that a firm's top earner should earn no more than 20 times what the lowest-ranked employee earns. What do you think?

 SOLUTION

This discussion should focus on three basic issues: the value of responsibility, the role of the market in determining wages, and social justice. The stance that an individual takes on this issue will depend on his or her view of the world. Those who support free-market economics may argue that executives are being paid for the value of the responsibility they have in their positions, that the pay scale is simply a matter of what the market requires, or that these upper-level positions have to be compensated in this way in order to retain competent and capable people. Others might argue that there is a need for some social justice and reasonableness, regardless of what the market will bear. No matter what your personal opinion may be, it is important that you understand the worldviews and values that cause others to take a different stance on this issue.

Designing a Compensation System

Most organizations design a compensation system that (1) enables the firm to achieve its strategic objectives and (2) is aligned with the firm's unique characteristics and environment. The objectives of developing successful compensation plans are to attract future candidates, motivate them to produce, and retain them in the organization.

In designing a compensation system, it is important to align payments with employee performance and help the organization create an environment and culture in which reward is based on exceptional performance. It is vital for the leaders of the organization to design the plan with its advantages and disadvantages of different types of plans in mind. Successful compensation plans are timely and expensive, and require commitment when they are being created and implemented. An important part of designing a compensation plan is to think of the different alternatives for monitoring performance and rewarding employees. Once the plan is in place, there needs to be constant and consistent monitoring of it, with supervisors and managers overseeing the evaluations of performance and using the system in the manner in which it was designed.

Internal versus External Equity

Internal equity refers to the perceived fairness of the pay structure within a firm. The value that an employer places on the company's internal equity relates to each specific job. It is important that employees' perceived job value be high, as this will not only motivate them to be more productive, but also encourage them to follow the company's objectives.

External equity refers to the perceived fairness of an employer's pay relative to what other employers provide their employees for the same type of labor. Focusing on external equity helps organizations be more competitive in their compensation plan. Creation of competitive compensation plans can attract, and keep, the best job candidates. For companies to develop compensation plans that are competitive, they must measure the market in which they operate.

In considering internal versus external equity, managers can use two basic models: distributive justice and the labor market. With regard to distributive justice, some employees may compare their input/outcome ratio to those of employees of other firms (external equity), but most will compare their ratios to those of their peers in the same organization (internal equity). According to the labor market model, the wage rate for an occupation is set at the point where the supply of labor equals the demand for labor in the marketplace. Thus, external equity is achieved when the firm pays its employees competitively *or* the "going rate" for the type of work they do.

Fixed versus Variable Pay

Variable pay is a pay scale that fluctuates according to some preestablished criterion, usually involving the experience the employee has or how long he or she has worked for the organization. Fixed pay is a form of pay that provides a predictable monthly paycheck and is the rule in the majority of U.S. organizations largely because it reduces the risk to both the employer and the employee.

For certain employee groups, such as sales, variable pay can be as high as 100 percent of compensation. The higher the percentage of variable pay, the more risk sharing there is between the employee and the firm. This form of variable pay is common in markets where it is important to sell high volumes of a product or service. Employees are compensated based on the objectives they reach and the goals they achieve, and are rewarded by their employers for greater performance. Employees in this model may receive lower fixed pay than other employees in the same firm or elsewhere. However, with variable pay and risk sharing between employee and employer, such employees can end up receiving a similar or greater amount of total compensation once the variable pay is added to the fixed base pay.

Performance versus Membership

The performance-versus-membership option is related to fixed versus variable pay. Firms that emphasize performance-contingent compensation may use piece-rate plans (in which payment is based solely on the number of units produced), cost-saving suggestion systems (in which employee suggestions that result in cost reductions lead to an increased salary for the employee making the suggestion), sales commissions, bonuses for perfect attendance, or merit pay. Firms that choose these forms of compensation promote competition among the employees within the organization, which can have both positive and negative effects. Competition may improve the numbers for the organization, but it may also lead to conflict among employees. If specific employees are consistently outperformed by others, they may feel that they are being undervalued, and this may cause them to perform at an even lower level or possibly to leave the company. If organizations choose one of these compensation strategies, continual communication must be maintained with all employees, not just the top performers, emphasizing how successful they all are making the organization. Furthermore, employees should feel that management or advisors are there to help them improve their personal performance, not only for their own gain, but for the company as a whole as well. Where the emphasis is on performance, rewards are tied directly to doing a better job, innovation, productivity, and profitability.

Firms that emphasize membership-contingent compensation provide the same wage to every employee in a given job. Employees may be paid by time (hours of work) and salary progression. This type of compensation promotes teamwork. When your compensation strategy is based on equality among employees, however, you may find a lack of willingness on the part of workers to exceed the required tasks and standards of the job.

The decision on whether to have a performance-based or membership-based compensation plan is related to how you want the internal structure of your firm organized. The relative emphasis on performance versus membership also depends largely on the company's culture and beliefs.

Job versus Individual Pay

Job-based compensation is a system based on the value or contributions of each job, not of the individual. Under such a system, the job is the unit of analysis for determining base compensation. The value of each job is set independently of the individual in that position. A problem with this type of compensation is that the individual in the job may feel undervalued or as if he or she cannot move within the company based on his or her skills or performance. Job pay in this system is dependent upon the market and the competitive rate that other firms may be offering for a similar position elsewhere. Based on these two factors, an organization will offer fair compensation relative to the job. Organizations are typically not seeking exceptional performance in these positions, only that the job be accomplished. When organizations pay by the job, the job is usually standardized within the industry, and the employees in these positions move up through the company over time. Job-based pay seems to work best in situations where the technology is stable, jobs do not change often, turnover is low, and training is required to do the job.

The individual pay system is quite the opposite of job-based compensation, emphasizing the individual rather than the job. Offspring of this concept include knowledge-based or skill-based pay systems, in which employees' pay is based either upon the specific job they can perform or upon the talents they can successfully apply to a variety of tasks and situations. When organizations pay based on the individual, they are hiring people who have high-level skills and who are motivated to learn, grow, and develop further abilities that will help the company. If an individual has a high skill level and is motivated to perform in the interests of the organization, this individual will receive better pay. Individual pay is used when organizations have a well-educated workforce and when the costs of turnover are high. Organizations want to reward the individuals that consistently perform well with greater compensation so that they stay with the company. Whether a firm should use job or individual pay depends on the prevailing conditions at that firm.

Elitism versus Egalitarianism

An elitist pay system establishes different compensation plans for different organizational levels and/or employee groups. Such pay structures tend to result in a more stable workforce because upward progression in the firm depends mostly on seniority. These hierarchical systems encourage employees to grow and move up within the organization. While elitist systems are more prevalent in stable environments, egalitarian systems are found more commonly in competitive environments.

An egalitarian pay system places most of the employees under the same compensation plan. During the 1990s, there was a trend toward this type of compensation system, which increased the possibilities of professional career growth and kept the status-related perks to a minimum. Egalitarian pay systems are usually more flexible than elitist ones and help to reduce or eliminate issues between employees related to pay based on an individual's status. This setup means that a traditional hierarchy will not be present. The choice between elitism and egalitarianism is a major one, as it creates an impression of what is necessary to succeed in the firm and perform the type of work that managers value.

Below-Market versus Above-Market Compensation

Below-market versus above-market compensation decisions are critical because of their influence on a firm's ability to attract workers, reduce employee turnover, and contain labor costs. When you underpay your employees, you may either lose talent or create resentment within the organization. Today more than ever, people understand what they and their work are "worth," and when organizations undervalue them, this can create problems. Organizations need to study the market so that they are prepared to deal with the consequences of their compensation choices, then they need to think long term when deciding to offer below-, above-, or at-market compensation to future employees. At-market wages are typical in industries that are both well-established and highly competitive. Firms paying below market tend to be small, young, and nonunionized.

When organizations offer above-market compensation, they usually have less difficulty in attracting highly qualified applicants, motivating their workforce, and retaining valued employees. Even with above-market compensation, however, it is not always guaranteed that the organization will perform better. If a firm offers below-market compensation, it may experience higher training costs because of its inability to retain employees. It may therefore benefit the company to hire employees with better compensation in the beginning to alleviate some of these costs overall. In general, above-market pay policies are more prevalent among larger companies in less competitive industries and among companies that have been performing well and therefore have the ability to pay more. Unionization is also a factor (see Chapter 13 for more information on this).

Monetary versus Nonmonetary Rewards

Monetary rewards include cash and forms of compensation that can be converted into cash at some future point (e.g., stock or pension plans). Nonmonetary rewards are intangibles, such as interesting work, challenging assignments, job security, and public recognition. While pay symbolizes what the organization values and signals to employees what activities are encouraged, organizations must decide how much emphasis to place on money and how much to place on other rewards. Generally, companies that emphasize monetary rewards want to reinforce individual achievement and responsibility, while those that emphasize nonmonetary rewards prefer to reinforce commitment to the organization.

Both monetary and nonmonetary rewards are tools that organizations use to motivate their employees to be more productive. Monetary rewards show the firm's appreciation in the form of cash, and nonmonetary rewards do so by providing opportunities to deserving employees based on their performance. Just as companies have to decide on what type of reward to give their employees for the betterment of the organization, they also need to consider which type of reward is best for the employee. Some employees are better off with monetary rewards, and some would prefer alternative payment options in the form of increased opportunities or other intangibles.

There are issues related to both monetary and nonmonetary rewards. For example, monetary rewards may motivate employees to do only what will lead to the incentive, instead of doing what is better for the organization and its members. Money can, and will, cause conflict between people, and, because of this, nonmonetary rewards and incentives need to be balanced in the organization and communicated effectively throughout the company. While both monetary and nonmonetary rewards are commonplace, rewards such as an extra day off or public recognition often prove to be cost-effective and have strong motivational powers within the organization.

Open versus Secret Pay

Some firms require employees to sign an oath that they will not divulge their monetary compensation to coworkers. This system is known as secret pay. The penalty for breaking the oath is termination. In other cases, known as open pay, employees' pay is a matter of public record. Open pay has two advantages: (1) it reduces pay dissatisfaction by providing open access to compensation information, and (2) it fosters fairness and greater motivation in climates that nurture employee relations. Many organizations utilize both systems: they do not publish individual salary or wage data, but they may provide information on pay and salary ranges if requested.

Though promoting fairness is the goal of making salaries open, this is not always achieved. Some say that when coworkers get upset over what another employee is receiving, this is good because the complaint is out in the open where it can be dealt with. However, secret pay might provide an added level of comfort for high-wage employees. It should be noted that most employees want only to be compensated fairly, not at a level that makes them the subject of jealousy and potential ridicule.

Companies have to educate their employees on what needs to be done to reach certain salary levels, as well as why some people receive higher compensation than others.

Most people consider their salary to be a personal and private affair. Therefore, organizations need to take into consideration how employees feel about their salaries being known by others. If employees feel that they are being compensated appropriately, and that such information should be shared only between them and the organization, conflict may occur under the open-pay system. A potential way for an organization to deal with such an issue is by posting a range of possible salaries for each job within the company, but not including specific employees' names. In this way, employees know what they will receive if they move up within the company. They will then concentrate on their own performance, instead of focusing on particular employee salaries.

Centralization versus Decentralization of Pay Decisions

With centralized pay systems, pay decisions are tightly controlled in a central location, normally the HR department at corporate headquarters. This system is more appropriate when it is cost-effective and efficient to hire compensation specialists, when the firm faces frequent legal challenges, and when there is a strong need to control expenses. Many organizations utilize a centralized pay system to be consistent in their rewards and incentives throughout the company in an effort to improve employee performance. Centralized systems, however, do not handle external equity concerns very well. Often these systems simply look internally to equalize pay levels, thus creating the possibility of losing valuable employees to competitors. As a result, large and diverse organizations are better served by a decentralized pay system.

A decentralized system delegates pay decisions throughout the firm, normally to unit managers. Decentralized systems operate better when an organization has many strategic objectives and is highly competitive in different markets. Decentralized pay systems are more responsive and more involved in what is going on in each individual unit of the organization. It should be noted, however, that more and more companies are moving to a centralized pay system in an attempt to be more effective and cut the costs of implementing these decentralized structures.

 Still Struggling

Creating an appropriate compensation "mix" is difficult and should be thought of as an iterative process. Typically the best resource in developing a new compensation plan, or updating a current one, is your existing employees. Ask employees what they like, what they don't like, what confuses them, what would make salary decisions more transparent, and any other questions that relate to their personal preferences with regard to compensation plans. Most suggestions will be easy to implement and relatively inexpensive!

Compensation Tools

Compensation tools are techniques that are used, simply put, to decide who should get paid what. The goal of these tools is to produce equitable payment systems that allow the firm to attract, retain, and motivate workers while keeping labor costs under control. These compensation tools fall into two categories: (1) job-based approaches and (2) skill-based approaches.

Job-Based Compensation Plans

Job-based plans are the most traditional and widely used ones. The primary objective of these plans is to allocate pay so that the most important jobs that command the highest earnings in the labor market are paid the most. The three key components of developing job-based plans are as follows:

1. *Achieving internal equity.* Internal equity is achieved through job evaluation, which involves job analysis, job descriptions, job specifications, rating of jobs, compensable factors, and establishment of job hierarchies.
2. *Achieving external equity.* External equity is achieved primarily through market surveys with benchmark jobs and payment policies.
3. *Achieving individual pay equity.* Individual pay equity is based on within-pay-range positioning criteria. This might be a case where individuals with varied experience levels are paid within a specified range, but at different levels. For example, if the pay range were $35,000–$45,000, an employee with five years' experience might receive a salary of $42,000, whereas a new hire with only one year of closely related experience might receive $37,000.

Skill-Based Compensation Plans

Skill-based compensation plans are far less common than job-based compensation plans. In skill-based plans, workers are paid based on how flexible they are or how capable of performing multiple tasks. The greater the variety of job-related skills that workers possess, the more they will be paid. Thus, a skill, rather than the job, is the unit of analysis. All employees start at the same pay rate and advance one pay level for each new skill that they master. There are basically three types of skills that employees may acquire: (1) depth skills, in which an employee becomes an expert in a given field, (2) breadth skills, in which an employee learns a number of jobs within a given firm, and (3) vertical skills, in which an employee acquires self-management abilities. Skill-based pay creates a more flexible workforce, promotes cross-training, calls for less overhead (supervisors), and increases employees' control over their output and, thus, their compensation. However, such a plan is not a panacea. To avoid cost overruns, perceptions of unfairness, and a highly regimented system, managers must carefully fit a skill-based system into their entire HR strategy.

When constructing a skill-based compensation system, organizations and their HR departments must first create a list of skill requirements needed for a job, establishing both current, necessary skills and future skills that an employee must acquire if he or she is to advance within the company. Next, all of these skills, as well as any others that current employees already have, must be inventoried. Based on this inventory, each skill should be assigned a value to create a pay structure. Unless a company is lucky enough to hire all of its employees with these skills already intact, the firm will have to implement training programs to help individuals develop the trades and tools needed to perform the organization's required work and meet its overall objectives.

The Legal Environment and Pay System Governance

The legal framework exerts a substantial amount of influence on the design and administration of compensation systems. The key federal laws that govern compensation criteria and procedures are the Fair Labor Standards Act, the Equal Pay Act, and the Internal Revenue Code, along with other state laws.

The Fair Labor Standards Act, 1938

The Fair Labor Standards Act (FLSA) is the fundamental compensation law in the United States and is administered by the Wage and Hour Division of the Department of Labor. The act is also referred to as the wage and hours bill because it sets the minimum wage (the lowest allowable wage that can be paid) and the maximum number of hours for nonexempt jobs. Today, the federal minimum wage is $7.25 per hour. Many states have their own minimum wage, and an employee is entitled to whichever of the two rates is higher.

The act also sets the standard for overtime pay. Covered nonexempt employees must receive overtime pay for time worked over 40 hours per workweek (the workweek is defined as any fixed and regularly recurring period of 168 hours, or seven consecutive 24-hour periods) at a rate no less than 1½ times the regular pay rate. There is no limit on the number of hours that employees

16 years of age or older may work in any workweek. The FLSA does not require this additional pay for work on weekends, holidays, or regular days of rest, unless overtime is worked on such days.

Recordkeeping and child labor standards are also set by the FLSA. In total, all of these standards affect more than 130 million workers, both full-time and part-time, in the private and public sectors. Most businesses are covered by the FLSA, except those with only one employee or annual gross sales of under $500,000.

The act applies to enterprises with employees who engage in interstate commerce; produce goods for interstate commerce; or handle, sell, or work on goods or materials that have been moved in or produced for interstate commerce. The act also covers the following regardless of their dollar volume of business: hospitals; institutions primarily engaged in the care of the sick, aged, mentally ill, or disabled who reside on the premises; schools for children who are mentally or physically disabled or gifted; preschools, elementary and secondary schools, and institutions of higher education; and federal, state, and local government agencies.

The Equal Pay Act, 1963

The Equal Pay Act (EPA) amends the FLSA and prohibits sex-based wage discrimination. The act requires that men and women be paid equally in jobs that are equal to one another. However, the EPA has four exceptions: (1) seniority, (2) level of performance, (3) quantity and quality of work, and (4) factors other than gender, such as race, ethnicity, and religion. If a company has pay differentials that are not covered by one of the four exceptions, it may face stiff penalties in the form of legal costs and back pay.

> **MINIMUM WAGE**
>
> **Secton. 206. (d) Prohibition of sex discrimination**
>
> (1) No employer having employees subject to any provisions of this section shall discriminate, within any establishment in which such employees are employed, between employees on the basis of sex by paying wages to employees in such establishment at a rate less than the rate at which he pays wages to employees of the opposite sex in such establishment for equal

work on jobs the performance of which requires equal skill, effort, and responsibility, and which are performed under similar working conditions, except where such payment is made pursuant to (i) a seniority system; (ii) a merit system; (iii) a system which measures earnings by quantity or quality of production; or (iv) a differential based on any other factor other than sex: Provided, That an employer who is paying a wage rate differential in violation of this subsection shall not, in order to comply with the provisions of this subsection, reduce the wage rate of any employee.

(2) No labor organization, or its agents, representing employees of an employer having employees subject to any provisions of this section shall cause or attempt to cause such an employer to discriminate against an employee in violation of paragraph (1) of this subsection.

(3) For purposes of administration and enforcement, any amounts owing to any employee which have been withheld in violation of this subsection shall be deemed to be unpaid minimum wages or unpaid overtime compensation under this chapter.

(4) As used in this subsection, the term "labor organization" means any organization of any kind, or any agency or employee representation committee or plan, in which employees participate and which exists for the purpose, in whole or in part, of dealing with employers concerning grievances, labor disputes, wages, rates of pay, hours of employment, or conditions of work.

The EPA protects equal pay for equal work, but it should not be confused with comparable worth. Comparable worth calls for comparable pay for jobs that are comparable in skills, effort, responsibility, and working conditions, even though the job content is different. These might include jobs at the same "pay grade" but with significantly different duties.

The Internal Revenue Code

The Internal Revenue Code (IRC) affects how much of their earnings employees take home. The IRC requires a company to withhold a portion of each employee's income to meet federal tax obligations. An employer's failure to comply with IRC requirements may result in wasted payroll dollars. Employees may also become frustrated with more complicated personal tax returns, large tax refunds (that might otherwise have been distributed throughout the year), and confusing tax liabilities.

PROBLEM 6-2

According to a consultant, the quality of many surveys on employee compensation and attitudes is low, in part because firms are deluged with requests from consulting companies to complete such surveys in exchange for access to the information provided by the survey. The result is that firms fill out surveys carelessly or do not respond to many of the surveys at all. Instead of using more experienced HR compensation specialists to complete surveys, firms often assign the task to entry-level HR employees or even clerical personnel. Therefore, the responses provided may not be as thorough or complete as they are when surveys are completed by more experienced professional staff. As a manager, how would you know if the salary survey data are accurate?

SOLUTION

It is hard to tell if the data are accurate unless the manager using the aggregate data has considerable knowledge of the benchmarking data provided by the companies participating in the survey. One way of checking is to contact the company that conducted the survey and ask it questions about the survey participants and any data that look questionable.

Chapter Summary

Compensation is much more than just the actual salary paid to an employee. In many cases, the level of compensation afforded an employee affects that employee's self-worth, commitment to the organization, and value as a member of the organization. Typically, firms provide their employees with other forms of compensation in addition to monetary ones. For this reason, it is important for the firm to properly communicate to employees how valuable these other forms of compensation might be to the employee. Furthermore, by continually understanding the labor market and the level of equity needed by the employees, HR managers can maintain high satisfaction and commitment by keeping pay levels in sync with the competitive landscape.

QUIZ

1. Which of the following is not a component of indirect employee compensation?
   A. Insurance
   B. Vacation
   C. Unemployment
   D. Bonus

2. When an employer makes sure that its employees are receiving pay similar to that received by individuals in similar positions in other organizations, it is making sure that there is _____ in pay levels.
   A. internal equity
   B. egalitarianism
   C. external equity
   D. fairness

3. Typically, commission-based employees are compensated via
   A. Variable-pay systems.
   B. Fixed-pay systems.
   C. Risk-versus-reward pay systems.
   D. Benefits-only pay systems.

4. This is a pay system that places most of the employees under the same compensation plan.
   A. Elitism
   B. Egalitarianism
   C. Below-market compensation
   D. Above-market compensation

5. The Fair Labor Standards Act of 1938 addresses all but which of the following?
   A. Minimum wage
   B. Gender wage discrimination
   C. Overtime pay
   D. Child labor provisions

6. When employees are compensated fairly relative to the entire job market, the firm has achieved what sort of equity?
   A. External
   B. Internal
   C. External and internal
   D. Market-level

7. Your company hires a new marketing manager. This position is typically paid $45,000/year; however, the new hire is offered and accepts $60,000/year based on his expertise and experience. Your firm is now using
   A. Job-based pay.
   B. Individual-based pay.
   C. Internal equity.
   D. Wage discrimination.

8. Which of the following is an advantage of an open pay system?
   A. Pay decisions are always equitable.
   B. Employee relations are nurtured through open access to information.
   C. There is general distrust of management.
   D. Individual employees can "opt out" of pay disclosure.

9. Which of the following is not one of the three key components of developing job-based plans?
   A. Achieving internal equity
   B. Achieving team-based equity
   C. Achieving external equity
   D. Achieving individual equity

10. Which of the following is not one of the basic types of skills that employees can acquire in skill-based compensation plans?
    A. Depth skills
    B. Vertical skills
    C. Horizontal skills
    D. Breadth skills

chapter 7

Benefits

Although benefits can be a significant asset to a firm's employees, they can also create a major headache for the untrained HR professional. In this chapter, we will shed some light on the different types of benefits your organization might offer, what options your firm might have for offering benefits, what types of benefits are required by law, and how the "benefits mix" can be helpful in retaining valued employees.

CHAPTER OBJECTIVES

After completing this chapter, the reader should be able to

1. Understand the "benefits mix" and the costs associated with benefits.

2. Understand legally required benefits and how they differ from other employee benefits.

3. Understand how benefits can be used to retain and motivate employees.

An Overview of Benefits

Employee benefits are referred to as indirect compensation. They are rewards for group membership that complement the base-pay and incentive-pay components of total compensation. Benefits provide services or facilities that are valued by many employees and that protect them from risks that could jeopardize their health and financial security. Employees with children, for example, will typically look for benefits that will further support their family, such as medical, vision, and dental benefits. Some employees will even sacrifice base salary for improved benefits, since the value of the benefits may outweigh the additional salary. Overall, benefits are considered the "extras" that employees receive on top of their salary.

Basic Terminology

When you are discussing benefits with employees, you may feel as if you are speaking a different language. In order to make you feel more comfortable discussing the concepts behind employee benefits, you should familiarize yourself with the following terms:

1. *Contributions* are payments to an annuity or retirement plan. Usually companies will contribute an amount of money to an employee's retirement account that is proportional to the amount the employee has contributed.

2. *Coinsurance* may be paid by your organization, with you and your employer splitting the cost of insurance benefits. Depending on how much the employee wants to pay to receive specific benefits, a company may pay for all of an employee's insurance or only a part of it. Alternatively, a company may cover all of an employee's personal insurance costs, but only a portion of his or her family's. It is important that you, as an HR representative, are familiar with your company's coinsurance policies so that you can accurately explain them to employees.

3. A *deductible* is the amount of the total cost that the employee is responsible for paying before insurance pays the remainder. The size of a particular employee's deductible can vary based on the plan that the employee has chosen, the services that he or she needs, and other issues such as monthly premiums and providers of choice.

4. *Flexible benefit programs* are set up so that employees can choose a plan that works best for them. Some or all of these programs can be tax-advantaged.

Employees may receive these benefits through contributions from the employer, direct monetary payment, or general insurance benefits.

The Cost of Benefits in the United States

The average amount paid by businesses in the form of benefits per hour was around $9 in March 2010. These benefits consist primarily of health insurance, paid vacation, and retirement savings plans.

Types of Benefits

The most common types of benefits are medical, retirement, insurance, and vacation. Benefits are expensive, and organizations need to take this into consideration when designing compensation plans for their employees. Some common options that are not legally required, but are fairly standard in most professions, are

- *Health insurance.* Although organizations are not legally required to provide health insurance to employees, many do provide this benefit. Depending on the organization, it may pay all or part of the cost of this insurance. There is usually a large group discount associated with receiving insurance through your company, so, for an individual employee, it is usually less expensive than buying one's own outside of the company's plan.
- *Retirement.* Retirement income is probably the largest benefit that employees receive. After they are vested with the company and have reached the designated retirement age, employees can begin to collect this benefit.
- *Life insurance.* This is usually paid for by the employer, but contributions from the employee may be required as well. Employees are often able to purchase extra coverage if they deem it necessary.
- *Paid time off.* Employees may accrue vacation time while they are with their company, receiving days or even weeks off. They are paid as if they were working their regular hours.

While not as common, some firms offer employee benefits such as on-site day care for employees' children, a gym, a cafeteria, and various subsidies for other services that the employee might require.

The Benefits Strategy

An effective benefits package, or strategy, needs to be aligned with the company's overall compensation strategy. The benefits mix is the complete package of benefits that a company chooses to offer to its employees. The benefits chosen govern the percentage of the total compensation package that will be allocated to benefits compared to the other components of the package (i.e., base salary and pay incentives). Flexibility of benefits choice is concerned with the degree of freedom that the employer gives its employees to tailor the benefits package to their personal needs. The benefits mix, amount, and flexibility provide a blueprint for designing the benefits package.

 PROBLEM 7-1

Most larger employers provide some sort of retirement fund for their employees. Do you think that companies are ethically bound to offer this benefit? Does the financial condition or size of the firm make any difference to your analysis?

 SOLUTION

While many larger employers do provide a retirement fund for their employees, many smaller employers may not have the financial resources or the expertise and techniques to do so. Practical considerations may make it impossible to offer these funds, especially in industries that utilize transient workers. However, an argument could be made that employers have an ethical and social responsibility to encourage their workers to participate in IRAs or other types of retirement plans that are available to the individual. Where possible, employers should offer payroll deductions for these plans.

The Benefits Mix

The benefits mix will depend on both the company's strategy and how badly it wants to recruit and retain the most qualified employees. In addition to the more basic benefits such as health insurance, retirement, and vacation time, an employer may include the following as further incentives:

- Tuition assistance or reimbursement (typically to help develop the skills and abilities of the company's employees, for the improvement of the organization)

- Child care (assistance or reimbursement)
- Health and physical fitness centers
- Elder care
- Flexibility with schedules
- Paid sick leave
- Maternity leave

Still Struggling

"Cafeteria" approaches to benefits (plans in which employees select the level and types of coverage they would like) are becoming more and more popular. Allowing employees to select from a set of options provides maximum flexibility. It should be noted that offering a variety of options often is not feasible for smaller companies; however, the attractiveness of even the smallest "benefit" should not be ignored, as benefits sometimes make a big difference in an employee's decision to accept or decline a job offer. Again, communication with employees is key in this area.

Legally Required Benefits

With only a few exceptions, all U.S. employers are legally required to provide social security, workers' compensation, and unemployment insurance. A fourth legally required benefit has been added in recent years: employers must offer unpaid leave to employees facing certain family and medical circumstances.

Social Security

Social security provides (1) income for retirees, the disabled, and survivors of deceased workers and (2) health care for the aged through the Medicare program. The components of social security are

- *Retirement income.* The amount of money you receive in retirement income depends on how much you earned throughout your career and at what age you begin collecting the benefits.

- *Disability income.* Depending on how long and how recently an employee has worked at a company, he or she can receive such benefits, which will start five months after the disability is incurred.

- *Medicare.* Medicare is primarily an insurance program for people 65 years of age or older, although individuals with disabilities who are under the age of 65 can also qualify. This program is financed by a portion of payroll taxes as well as monthly premiums taken from social security checks.

- *Survivor benefits.* If a worker who is covered by social security dies, his or her spouse can receive benefits.

Workers' Compensation

Workers' compensation (colloquially known as "workers' comp" in North America) is a form of insurance that provides medical care, income continuation, and rehabilitation expenses for people who sustain job-related injuries or illnesses, in exchange for mandatory relinquishment of the employee's right to sue his or her employer for the tort of negligence. Workers' compensation also provides income to the survivors of an employee whose death is job-related.

State workers' compensation laws have no safety regulations or mandates, but they do require employers to pay for workers' compensation insurance.

There are three major components of workers' compensation:

- *Medical expense.* This consists of any expenses incurred as a result of an injury while on the job and is the responsibility of the employer.

- *Disability pay.* If an injury while working results in disability, the employer may be responsible for paying the injured employee anywhere from $1/2$ to $2/3$ of his or her original salary during the time that the employee is unable to work.

- *Vocational rehabilitation.* Employers may be liable to pay for retraining or physical therapy if an injury on the job has rendered an employee unable to perform specific functions.

The costs of workers' compensation to the employer can be very high, especially if the organization incurs penalties related to any unsafe working conditions that may have resulted in the injury of an employee or employees. The best way to prevent such a situation is to provide a safe environment for everyone in the organization, including proper safety training for all staff members.

Unemployment Insurance

Unemployment insurance (UI) provides people with temporary income during periods of involuntary unemployment. The program is part of a national wage stabilization policy, evolved from the Wage Stabilization Policy implemented by President Truman in 1945, that is designed to steady the economy during recessionary periods. When the economy is doing well, there are a greater number of people working, causing more money to be contributed to UI. These payments when the economy is healthy create a cushion, so that during times of recession, money is available for the unemployed. People receiving these benefits are then able to help strengthen the economy by putting money back into it.

Unpaid Leave

The Family and Medical Leave Act of 1993 (FMLA) now requires most employers to provide eligible employees with up to 12 weeks of unpaid leave for the following reasons:

- Birth of a child
- Adoption of a child
- Care for a sick spouse, child, or parent
- The employee's own serious health problems
- Care for an injured service member in the family
- Addressing qualifying exigencies arising out of a family member's deployment

The FMLA also requires that employees be able to return to the same position that they held when they went on leave. If the position is occupied, then the company must offer the returning employee a job that is equal in terms of pay and function. All of an employee's benefits will be protected and will be reinstated when the employee returns. Protection from employer retaliation is also provided.

Voluntary Benefits

Health insurance is one of the voluntary benefits that employees value most. It provides health-care coverage for employees and often for their dependents as well, protecting them from possible financial disaster in the event of a serious illness or injury. Retirement plans can also be considered a voluntary benefit, as can life and disability insurance, paid time off, and specific employee services (e.g., tuition assistance and reimbursement).

Health Insurance

There are three common types of employer-provided health insurance plans: (1) traditional health insurance, (2) health maintenance organizations (HMOs), and (3) preferred provider organizations (PPOs).

Traditional health insurance allows the employee to go to any doctor, change doctors, and receive coverage nationwide. These plans, however, are more expensive than other programs because of the abundance of flexibility.

Health maintenance organizations (HMOs) provide health-care services from doctors and hospitals with which the HMO has a contract. HMOs cover only treatments provided by these doctors and hospitals. Because of the Health Maintenance Organization Act of 1973, businesses employing more than 25 employees must offer federally certified HMO options if they offer medical insurance at all.

Preferred provider organizations (PPOs) are similar to HMOs, but they allow an employee to seek treatment outside of the designated doctors and hospitals as long as he or she pays for any additional costs. For instance, if an employee has a primary-care physician that he or she wants to stay with when transferring to a new company, the new PPO will cover the cost up to the amount that it would have paid if the employee had visited one of its designated primary-care physicians. The employee then pays any outstanding difference.

Retirement Benefits

In today's economic environment, retirement benefits are often the first benefits eliminated by firms that are looking to contain costs. The days when any professional-level position meant a guaranteed pension are no more. However, there are still many beneficial, generous, and easy-to-use retirement benefits options for employees.

The Employment Retirement Income Security Act (ERISA) was established to ensure that at least some minimum standard exists for employees who are establishing a form of retirement savings. This federal law sets minimum standards for voluntarily established pension and health plans in private industry to provide protection for the individuals involved. This legislation works in a way similar to the FDIC (the federal program designed to protect deposits in banks) in that it does not require a minimum level of benefits, but it does guarantee the solvency and safety of an individual's investment in such a plan. Additionally, ERISA does not require companies to provide health insurance, but it regulates the operation of health benefits if a company does establish health insurance.

Defined-benefit plans are the traditional "pension plans" that provide a set level of income after retirement, based on an employee's length of service with an organization. Many times, defined-benefit plans offer better retirement benefit options than other retirement packages, especially if employees live to a very old age. The downside, however, is that few private employers still offer these plans (although most state, local, and federal government employees qualify for this type of plan). The investment decision-making responsibility in this plan rests with the employers, not the employees, and the organization is often more responsive to movements in the financial markets than individual employees would be.

Defined-contribution plans are retirement plans in which the firm contributes a certain amount of money for the employee to manage as retirement savings. Examples of defined-contribution plans are Individual Retirement Accounts (IRAs) (plans that individuals contribute to above and beyond their company-offered retirement plans), 401(k) plans (plans that provide employer matching funds for employee contributions), and 403(b) plans [plans that operate similar to a 401(k) but are offered to employees of educational and not-for-profit entities]. Many times the employer will encourage an employee to contribute his or her personal earnings to these plans by promising to "match" contributions up to a certain dollar value. For example, Company A will match an employee's contribution dollar for dollar up to 15 percent of the employee's gross salary. In essence, Company A is offering free money to the employee in the form of the employer's contribution to the employee's retirement fund. An additional benefit is that the employee's contribution is a "pretax" benefit that is not subject to income tax, effectively lowering the employee's taxable income. While the benefits are tremendous, tax law generally limits the amount of money that a person can contribute to each form of defined-contribution plan.

PROBLEM **7-2**

Assume that you run a small business. Visit the Web site www.dol.gov/elaws. Write a two-page summary explaining (1) the various retirement savings programs available to small-business employers, and (2) which retirement savings program you would choose for your small business and why.

 **SOLUTION**

Based on what you have learned from the chapter and the results of your Internet search, the plan should include, at a minimum, a 401(k) plan that can be accessed online.

Insurance Plans

A life insurance plan is a contract between the person who is insured and the company that is insuring him or her, stating that if the person dies, the company will pay a stated benefit to a beneficiary of the insured's choice. In return, the insured will pay into an account until he or she passes away or the plan is terminated.

Long-term disability insurance is set up to help people with the financial aspects of being unable to work for long periods of time. Some people may be able to live off of their savings or other non-work-related income, but many others need insurance to help in the event that a serious medical situation arises. Long-term disability insurance provides an employee with 50 to 60 percent of his or her salary, depending on the policy, for anywhere from two to five years or until the employee turns 65. Also depending on the policy, once an employee is considered disabled, he or she may no longer be required to pay premiums.

Paid Time Off

It is not currently a federal requirement for employers to provide employees with paid time off (either sick leave or vacation). However, under the Family and Medical Leave Act, unpaid sick leave is required.

Vacations are a type of paid time off that many organizations offer their employees. Paid vacations are earned through work performed, and normally accrue based on the number of years the employee has worked for the organization or the employee's job position.

Severance pay is intended to help employees financially while they are looking for other employment. Severance pay is provided in situations such as involuntary terminations or layoffs and may be given in installments or as a lump sum.

Holidays and other paid time off are benefits that some employees receive. Although federal employees receive holiday pay for time off, employees in the private sector are not entitled to receive this benefit. Private-sector employers are also not required to give employees time off, paid or unpaid, for holidays.

Administering Benefits

The use of flexible benefits and the importance of communicating benefit plans and options to employees are critical in the administration of employee benefits. A flexible benefits program allows employees to choose from a selection of employer-provided benefits; these may include vision care, dental care, health insurance coverage for dependents, additional life insurance coverage, long-term disability insurance, child care, elder care, additional paid vacation days, legal services, and contributions to a 401(k) retirement plan.

Many employees with excellent benefits packages have never been informed of the value of these benefits and are likely to underestimate their worth. By effectively communicating the importance of these benefits and educating employees on their worth, firms can enable employees to choose those benefits that fit their needs. Therefore, communication concerning benefits is essential.

Flexible Benefits

Flexible plans are often referred to as "cafeteria" plans, since employees can pick and choose the benefits that best fit their individual needs. There are two types of cafeteria plans: core-plus plans and modular plans. Core-plus plans have specific benefits that employees are required to take to meet their basic needs. In addition to these specific benefits, employees can purchase additional benefits that better fit their needs through a credit program. Modular plans might have three levels of benefits arranged in no specific categories that the employee is able to choose from. Module 1 may have three benefits in it, then module 2 has those three plus another benefit, and module 3 will have all of those benefits plus maybe two others. The employee then decides which module works best for his or her own personal situation.

There are problems associated with flexible plans, including that they are harder to establish. Organizations that provide employees with more options have to record and maintain records concerning the benefit plans that their employees choose. Communication is also an issue with regard to the explanation of the benefits themselves and of any changes in cost, coverage, or use of these benefits. When people's lives change, they may need to update or alter their benefits, contributing to an additional layer of potential communication failure. Since companies need to continually comply with the rules and regulations associated with the benefit plans, any changes in an employee's benefits must be made clear, not only to the employer, but to the employee as well.

PROBLEM 7-3

You are the HR consultant to a small business with about 40 employees. At the present time, the firm offers only five days' vacation, five paid holidays, and legally mandated benefits such as unemployment insurance payments. Develop a list of other benefits that you believe it should offer, along with your reasons for suggesting them.

SOLUTION

The specific recommendations would depend partly on the profile of the firm's employees. In the absence of that information, the least costly addition of benefits would be to add some sick leave (or personal days) and consider additional vacation or holidays. The next benefit that could be considered would be to make available some kind of health plan that could require a contributory cost from the employee. This option would be less expensive to the company and would be of real value to the employees because of the group discounts.

Chapter Summary

The world of benefits management can be confusing and frustrating. However, a skilled HR manager who understands the wants and needs of the firm's employees can create a benefits mix that provides the firm with a significant competitive advantage. It should not be overlooked that especially in today's labor market, total compensation (which includes benefits offered) is considerably more important than simply salary when employees are evaluating job offers. Through careful thought and research, your firm's benefits plan can be an easy route to organizational success.

QUIZ

1. **Which of the following is considered a defined-benefit plan?**
   A. IRA
   B. 401(k)
   C. Pension
   D. 403(b)

2. **Which of the following is not a legally required benefit?**
   A. Health insurance
   B. Social security
   C. Unemployment
   D. Workers' compensation

3. **The Family and Medical Leave Act of 1993 (FMLA) provides leave for all but which of the following reasons?**
   A. Birth and/or adoption of a child
   B. Care of a sick spouse, child, or parent
   C. The employee's own serious health problem
   D. Care of an employee's sick same-sex partner

4. **Severance pay is given in which of the following situations?**
   A. An employee quits.
   B. An employee retires.
   C. An employee is laid off.
   D. An employee is a high performer.

5. **ERISA provides**
   A. Federal protection of retirement assets.
   B. A guaranteed rate of return on retirement assets.
   C. An investment strategy for retirement funds.
   D. Government mandates for benefits coverage.

6. **Unemployment insurance**
   A. Is a legally required benefit.
   B. Is designed to pay 100 percent of a person's salary if that person loses his or her job.
   C. Provides temporary subsidies for people who are out of work.
   D. Both a and c.

7. **This program was established as a protection of rights to employee benefits.**
   A. Family and Medical Leave Act of 1993 (FMLA)
   B. Consolidated Omnibus Budget Reconciliation Act of 1985 (COBRA)
   C. Employee Retirement Income Security Act of 1974 (ERISA)
   D. Pension Protection Act of 2006

8. **Which of the following is not a component of workers' compensation?**
   A. Medical expense
   B. Educational assistance
   C. Vocational rehabilitation
   D. Disability pay

9. **Which of the following is true about defined-contribution retirement plans?**
   A. The employer guarantees a certain income upon retirement.
   B. The employer manages his or her retirement savings.
   C. The employee receives a sum of money that he or she can manage independently.
   D. The employee can withdraw his or her money at any time.

10. **Benefits**
    A. Are very expensive for firms, but provide great value and stability for employees.
    B. Are inexpensive and should be provided to any employee at any time.
    C. Are not legally required.
    D. Can sometimes force employees to leave their job.

Training and Development

This section covers the all too often confused topics of training and development. Although *training* is typically used in conjunction with *development*, the terms are not synonymous. Training typically focuses on providing employees with specific skills or helping them correct deficiencies in their performance. In contrast, development is an effort to provide employees with abilities that the organization will need if it is to grow, compete, and prosper in the future.

CHAPTER OBJECTIVES

After completing this chapter, the reader should be able to

1. Understand the difference between training and development.

2. Determine the type, amount, and nature of training and/or development needed in your organization.

3. Understand and describe the costs and benefits associated with both training and development.

4. Determine the type of development that is appropriate for employees in your organization.

Training

Upgrading employees' performance and improving their skills through training is a necessity in today's competitive environment. The training process brings with it many questions that managers must consider, starting with

- Is training the solution to the problem?
- Are the goals of training clear and realistic?
- Is training a good investment?
- Will the training work?

Answering these questions will help management identify whether issues that arise are due to a lack of training and problematic training processes or due to performance deficits. Management must then determine whether investing in training is the most appropriate solution to a particular issue.

 PROBLEM 8-1

Some companies reimburse the educational expenses of employees who take classes on their own. In an era in which people can count less and less on a single employer to provide them with work over the course of their careers, do you think employers have a responsibility to encourage their employees to pursue educational opportunities?

 SOLUTION

Probably the biggest point of contention in this question will be whether "encourage" means to pay for employees' education, as the question implies, or to counsel employees concerning further education and provide flexibility and accommodations when possible. It is unlikely that anyone would argue that employers do not have an ethical responsibility to *encourage* employees to pursue educational opportunities. There will probably be some disagreement, however, over whether or not an organization should *pay for* employees to take classes. Some employers simply are not large enough, or do not generate a great enough profit margin, to afford such undertakings. However, maybe the question should be, "If they can afford to do so, do they have the ethical responsibility to pay for employees' education?" There are significant differences of opinion on this topic related to employee retention rate, the employee-employer relationship,

personal beliefs with regard to the role of the employer, what courses will be taken and how they will affect an employee's performance, and many other considerations.

Is Training the Solution to the Problem?

Often training is used as a Band-Aid for organizational problems. Both employees and employers use lack of training as an excuse for other extant issues. Before implementing a training program to correct a problem, a critical analysis of *how* this training will fix the problem should be done. Is training actually the solution to the organization's problem, or can the problem be attributed to job design? Is it the qualifications of employees or the organizational design?

Are the Goals Clear and Realistic?

Management must determine what it would like the training session to accomplish. The goal should be articulated as clearly as possible and should be communicated to employees. It is also important that management be realistic about the goals. For example, if employees are required to learn a new finance application, management must determine whether one training session will suffice or whether multiple sessions will be required.

Is Training a Good Investment?

In addition to the tangible costs of a new training program, there are also other costs involved, like time spent away from completing core job functions. With economic conditions continuing to look grim, management must determine whether the training is cost-effective.

Will Training Work?

Training programs are typically not guaranteed to work; therefore, management must carefully consider all of the above-mentioned factors and determine what is right for the firm.

The Training Process

Effective training can raise performance, improve morale, and increase an organization's potential. Poor, inappropriate, or inadequate training can be a source of frustration for everyone involved. To maximize the benefits of training, managers must closely monitor the training process.

Assessment

The overall purpose of the assessment phase of the training process is to determine whether training is needed and, if it is, to provide the information required to design a training program. The objectives of training must be clarified, must be related to the KSAs (the knowledge, skills, and abilities necessary to be successful in a particular position) identified in the task analysis, and should be challenging, precise, achievable, and understood by all. Assessment consists of three levels: (1) organizational analysis, (2) task analysis, and (3) person analysis.

- *Organizational analysis.* This type of analysis examines major components of the organization, such as its mission, culture, overall goals, and structure. It is imperative to first determine what the organization needs in order to fulfill its mission and decide what type of training will fit with the organization's current culture. Also consider who should attend training, given the structure of the firm.

- *Task analysis.* Most simply put, task analysis examines the work that needs to be performed within the organization. Consider what specific tasks need to be trained and who will ideally be performing these tasks within the firm. What skills will these individuals need to acquire?

- *Person analysis.* This final type of analysis evaluates how well employees are completing their tasks and identifies those who may need additional training. Are the employees currently completing the appropriate and assigned tasks? If not, can current employees be trained to complete these tasks? If the answer is again no, then the firm may need to start from scratch, and rehiring and training the new people for the position.

Training and Conduct

The training program that results from assessment should be a direct response to an organizational problem or need. Approaches to these programs vary in terms of their location, presentation, and type.

1. *Location options.*
   - *On the job.* Under supervision and guidance, an employee learns to complete tasks in an actual work setting. An example of this type of training is an internship.

- *Off the job*. Training usually takes place in a classroom or alternative setting and is more formalized, such as taking a course outside of work.

2. *Presentation options.*
   - *Slides and videotapes*. This type of presentation uses visual and/or audio stimulation while presenting material.
   - *Teletraining*. This type of presentation uses technology such as Skype to train from an alternative location.
   - *Computers*. Many options are available with computers, including training by CD-ROM; over the Internet or an intranet; or through other types of e-learning.
   - *Simulations*. These offer a situation that replicates a real event.
   - *Virtual reality*. This presentation method is commonly used by the military for training.
   - *Classroom instruction and role plays*. These methods of presentation offer learning in a social environment.

3. *Types of training.*

   - *Skills training*. A training need is identified, then specific objectives and content are created to address that need. Once the training is finished, the trainees complete an assessment so that management can determine if the objective was accomplished.
   - *Retraining*. As the requirements of jobs change, employees can attend classes or programs to keep up with the business need, or even shadow another employee within a firm who may have the required skills.
   - *Cross-functional training*. This is training that provides employees with the skills needed to complete assignments that are not necessarily a regular job function, giving them a better idea of the bigger picture and helping them further understand work processes across the business.
   - *Team training*. This involves content tasks that are directly related to goals and group processes that address the functions of the team.
   - *Creativity training*. This largely involves the use of brainstorming as a technique to generate ideas; it is based on the assumption that creativity can be learned.
   - *Literacy training*. This type of training addresses basic math, reading, and writing skills.

- *Diversity training.* This type of training uses a culturally sensitive approach to teach employees about specific cultural and gender differences.
- *Crisis training.* This focuses on dealing with, and preventing, disastrous events.
- *Customer service training.* This teaches employees critical information about how to interact and deal with customers, especially when a customer is upset about an issue. Customer service is critical to the success of most businesses, whether for- or not-for-profit.

Evaluation

In this phase, the effectiveness of the training is assessed. Effectiveness can be measured in monetary or nonmonetary terms. It is important that the training be assessed on how well it addresses the needs that it was designed to address. Effectiveness can be measured by participants' reactions, participants' learning, and the company's return on the training investment.

Orientation and Socialization

Orientation is the process of informing new employees of what is expected of them in the job and helping them cope with the stresses of transition. It is possible that this is the most important training opportunity for many organizations, occurring when employees first start with the firm. Managers have the chance to set the tone for new employees at this time.

Socialization is the larger process of employee adjustment. The socialization process entails a naïve outsider entering the organization and learning its day-to-day operations, conventions, task-related and social-related activities, and political structures. The socialization process takes a much longer time period than is normally afforded for orientation.

 PROBLEM 8-2

Are companies ethically responsible for providing literacy training for workers who lack basic skills? Why or why not?

 SOLUTION

As with the previous question, a lot of the controversy on this issue may boil down to whether companies can afford to provide such training. In the case of literacy training, there are often many low- or no-cost alternatives available. There are government agencies that are interested in providing funds for this type of training, and there are foundations that will underwrite its costs. Local volunteer organizations are often involved in this type of training as well. A question to consider is, how can an organization fulfill its ethical responsibilities without necessarily incurring significant costs?

Development

Career development is an ongoing organized and formal effort that recognizes people as a vital resource. It differs from training in that it has a wider focus, a longer time frame, and a broader scope. The goal of training is improvement in performance; the goal of development is enrichment and the creation and nurturing of more capable workers.

Recently, career development has come to be seen as a means for meeting both organizational and employee needs, as opposed to solely meeting the needs of the organization, as it had done in the past. Now, organizations see career development as a way of preventing job burnout, providing employees with career mobility information, improving the quality of employees' work lives, and meeting affirmative action goals. Career development must be seen as a key business strategy if an organization wants to survive in an increasingly competitive and global business environment.

As you may have noticed, firms like Xerox, Enterprise, and Bank of America, among others, have come to be known as incubators for future talent. Their training and employee development programs are legendary for their quality and their ability to develop strong managers and leaders. The quality of these companies' programs leads potential employees to select their offers over those of competitors even though the salary they offer might be lower, as the potential for future success at these companies is tremendous.

 PROBLEM 8-3

How much responsibility does a company have for managing its employees' careers? Can a company take too much responsibility for its employees' career development? In what ways might this be harmful to employees?

 **SOLUTION**

It is clear that it is good management to have a career development plan for an employee's internal career. However, a company must still expect

employees to take some measure of responsibility for managing their own careers, both within and outside of the organization. The dangers in the employer's taking too much responsibility for career development include the potential loss of motivation and drive on the part of the employees, resentment by the employees of their loss of choices in their career path, and employees' utilization of developed career-oriented skills in a different position or at another company.

Challenges in Development

While most businesspeople today agree that their organizations should invest in their employees' career development, it is not always clear exactly what form this investment should take. Before implementing a career development program, management needs to consider the major challenges associated with career development discussed here.

Many modern organizations have concluded that employees must take an active role in creating and implementing their own personal development plans. There are a number of situations that lead companies to encourage their employees to take responsibility for their own development, including mergers, acquisitions, downsizing, and even the concept of employee empowerment. However, employees typically need at least some general guidance regarding the steps they can, and should, take to develop their careers, both within and outside of the company.

Too much emphasis on career enhancement can also harm an organization's effectiveness. Employees with an extreme career orientation can become more concerned about the next step up in their career and their general image than about their performance. Some warning signs that a manager should be on the lookout for, to avoid such a situation, include an employee's heavy focus on advancement opportunities, managing impressions, and socializing rather than job performance.

There are also serious side effects of career development programs if they foster unrealistic expectations for advancement, including employee dissatisfaction, poor performance, and job turnover.

Another challenge that companies potentially face is the difficulty in meeting the career development needs of today's diverse workforce. For example, in 1991, a government study revealed that women and members of minority groups were frequently excluded from informal career development activities such as networking, mentoring, and participation in policy-making committees. This trend has continued into the 2000s, creating a bottleneck in the career path for members of minority groups. Perhaps the best way a company can ensure that members of these groups have a fair chance of obtaining managerial and executive positions is to design a broad-based approach to employee development, anchored in education and training.

Another employee group that may need special consideration is dual-career couples. Common organizational approaches that are becoming increasingly popular in dealing with the needs of dual-career couples are flexible work schedules, telecommuting, and the offering of child-care services. Some companies have also been counseling couples in career management.

Regardless of the group, there will be challenges to face in employee development when deciding what programs to implement and how to implement them effectively. Management needs to consider the best options and practices that will allow the company to create a well-developed workforce in an increasingly diverse and ever-expanding workplace.

Creating an Effective Development Program

Creative decision making is a must in designing and implementing an effective development program. The three phases of development often blend together in a real-life program. These three phases are (1) assessment, (2) direction, and (3) development.

 PROBLEM 8-4

Explain the career-related factors to keep in mind when making an employee's first assignments.

 SOLUTION

Providing realistic job previews, challenging first jobs, and mentors can help prevent reality shock. Solutions should also focus on creating a connection with the organization. It is important to note that early career experiences shape the later behavior and attitudes of employees. With this in mind, it is important to provide employees with connection, autonomy, and excitement.

Assessment

The assessment phase of creating an effective development plan involves both self-assessment and organizationally provided assessment. The goal of both is to identify employees' strengths and weaknesses.

- *Self-assessment.* The major tools needed to complete a self-assessment are workbooks and workshops offered by firms specializing in self-assessment. Individuals might assess their personalities, job acuity, and interests in order to define their development plan. Using a workbook, an employee can identify policies, procedures, and information regarding his or her own career issues. Employees may also attend workshops to help them focus on their career aspirations and the strategies necessary for achieving these goals. Self-assessments involve skills-assessment exercises, interests inventories, and clarification of values. When an employer does not routinely offer development programs, it is essential that employees work out their own development plans. Planning for your career should include a consideration of how you can demonstrate that you make a difference to the organization.

- *Organizational assessment.* Performance appraisals and succession planning are examples of tools that organizations use in attempts to help employees develop their career. One of the key tools in organizational assessment is the "promotability forecast," in which managers evaluate the advancement potential of employees. Succession planning is also critical for the firm as a whole, especially when a company foresees any sort of retirement or vacancy on the horizon.

Direction

This phase involves determining the type of career that employees want and the steps they must take to make these career goals a reality.

- *Individual career counseling.* Meeting with a career counselor helps employees examine their personal career aspirations in a one-on-one setting. This type of counseling is helpful because it focuses directly on an individual and his or her specific career goals, as compared to a more general approach.

- *Information services.* Information services provide employees with the opportunity to explore their own career path by utilizing job postings, skills inventories, general profession and career information, and other useful career exploration and career-building tools.

PROBLEM 8-5

Choose three occupations (such as management consultant, HR manager, and salesperson) and use some of the online sources from the Department of Labor, www.salary.com, and job posting sites such as monster.com, jobing.com, and theladders.com to make an assessment of the future demand for each occupation in the next 10 years or so. Does each of them seem like a good occupation to pursue? Why or why not?

SOLUTION

Support your conclusions with data and information from these sources. For example, you might search monster.com and find 10 open postings for "HR manager"; then, when searching salary.com, you find that salaries for HR managers have been increasing over the past few years, even in a weak economy. It would seem that this job has the potential for great growth. Next, you look at the Department of Labor statistics on income and note that your geographic area has lower wages that many other metropolitan areas—this too could be an indicator that your area is ripe for economic development.

Development

The development phase of the program is one in which actions are taken to create and increase an employee's skills in preparation for future job opportunities. This phase is meant to foster an employee's growth and self-improvement, and there are a number of options for doing so.

- *Mentoring.* This is a relationship between a senior and an entry-level employee or a peer relationship that focuses on development, support, and networking.
- *Coaching.* This process involves an employee meeting with management, either regularly or spontaneously, to discuss career goals and development.
- *Job rotation.* This procedure allows employees to work in areas other than their own so that they can acquire additional work skills and decrease monotony.
- *Tuition assistance programs.* Through these programs, the employer offers monetary support for an employee's course or career development programs.

Still Struggling

Training and development can also be portrayed as benefits provided by the company. The value of training and development programs is often overlooked when "total compensation" is being discussed. Consider the costs and benefits associated with training and development before selecting programs and participants. It may be wise to require employees to sign long-term contracts or noncompete agreements before placing them in certain training programs.

Chapter Summary

Overall, training and development are essential to organizational effectiveness and employee satisfaction. For example, some applicants choose to work at certain firms simply because of the quality of their training and/or development programs. As you can see, training and development programs can be key in employee retention and motivation; however, these programs must be designed and administered appropriately. If your firm correctly identifies the need for and application of training and development programs, they can become a tremendous source of competitive advantage.

QUIZ

1. This is taking action to create and increase employees' skills to prepare them for future job opportunities and is meant to foster growth and self-improvement.
    A. Development phase
    B. Self-development
    C. Assessment phase
    D. Direction phase

2. This focuses on providing employees with specific skills or helping them to correct deficiencies in their performance.
    A. Training
    B. Development
    C. Conduct review
    D. Assessment

3. Which of the following is a key consideration for managers regarding the training process?
    A. Acknowledge that training will work.
    B. Determine whether training is a good investment.
    C. Set high expectations and goals for employees.
    D. Determine whether terminating employees is the solution.

4. Which of the following *is not a* level of assessment analysis?
    A. Organizational
    B. Task
    C. Paired
    D. Person

5. This involves determining the type of career that employees want and the steps that they must take to make their career goals a reality.
    A. Development phase
    B. Self-development
    C. Assessment phase
    D. Direction phase

6. An ongoing organized and formalized effort that recognizes people as a vital organizational resource is
    A. Coaching.
    B. Career development.
    C. Human resource management.
    D. Cross-functional training.

7. In the event that unrealistic expectations are created, serious side effects of career development programs include all but which of the following?
   A. Employee dissatisfaction
   B. Layoffs
   C. Turnover
   D. Poor performance

8. Organizations are increasingly offering dual-career couples which of the following?
   A. Telecommuting
   B. Child-care services
   C. Flexible work schedules
   D. All of the above

9. This involves activities ranging from self-assessment to organizationally provided assessment.
   A. Development phase
   B. Self-development
   C. Assessment phase
   D. Direction phase

10. Which of the following is the main goal of training?
    A. Improvement in performance
    B. Enrichment and more capable workers
    C. Neither a or b
    D. Both a and b

chapter 9

Performance Management and Appraisal

This chapter covers performance management and appraisal and examines several essential management functions, such as motivation and incentive plans. Issues of errors and bias are also explored. It is imperative that managers know how to get the most out of their employees as well as how to properly assess their performance. This chapter will give an overview of the basics in each area.

CHAPTER OBJECTIVES

After completing this chapter, the student should be able to

1. Understand common challenges in performance evaluation.

2. Understand and describe the impact of pay-for-performance plans.

3. Determine the type of performance management approach that is appropriate for his or her organization.

Performance Management and Appraisal Basics

When someone is searching for a job or deciding how to craft a position description, one of the primary dimensions discussed always seems to involve the concepts of performance management and performance appraisal, or, in more common parlance, "How do I move up and/or get a raise?" Human nature dictates that certain individuals are driven to perform, while others need a bit of a "push start" in order to get them moving in the right direction. This section will focus on some of the technical aspects of, as well as tips for, motivating, measuring, and, ultimately, improving performance in your organization.

While the terms are often used interchangeably, performance management and performance appraisal are two very different managerial responsibilities. Performance appraisal is an occasional (usually annual or semiannual) process in which an employee's performance, goals, and objectives are measured and evaluated. Performance management, on the other hand, is managers' almost daily task of getting the best work out of their employees, making them the most effective and efficient employees that they can be.

Performance appraisal involves the identification, measurement, and management of human performance in organizations. Organizations usually conduct appraisals for administrative (a decision about an employee's working conditions, including promotions and rewards) and/or developmental (a decision concerning strengthening the employee's job skills, including counseling and training) purposes. These appraisals, however, are typically met with a high level of dissatisfaction from all levels of an organization. HR professionals, line managers, and employees all voice concern. Many workers have difficulty with the appraisal process, which may account for the short life span of the average appraisal system within a company. When an appraisal system is poorly explained or poorly implemented, the individuals who perform the appraisals will quickly shift to less invasive or confusing methods. This situation can lead to inequity within the firm if different appraisal formats are used for different employees.

PROBLEM 9-1

Performance appraisal is a management tool. As such, managers often use this tool to benefit themselves or the company. For example, a manager may use overly positive performance ratings as a reward for someone who spearheaded a project for the manager. Likewise, a manager may use overly harsh ratings as punishment for someone who objected to a project that the manager promoted. Do you think this use of the appraisal system is acceptable? Why or why not?

SOLUTION

If consciously performed, this behavior is unethical. However, the likelihood is that the manager really believes that the performance ratings that she or he provided were accurate. The problem with performance appraisals is that our biases and many other factors affect how we view someone at a particular point in time. Thus, if we are upset with someone, we are likely to think of him or her as a lower performer. If we are pleased with someone, we are likely to think more highly of his or her performance.

Identifying Performance

The first step in the performance appraisal process is for managers to identify the aspects or dimensions of performance that are to be measured. This measurement provides the manager with an understanding of how effective job performance occurs. The process may seem simple, but it can be quite complicated. If a significant dimension is missing, employee morale may suffer because employees who do well on that dimension will not be recognized or rewarded for their specific strengths. If an irrelevant or trivial dimension is included, employees may perceive the whole appraisal process as meaningless.

Measuring employee performance involves assigning numbers or labels (e.g., excellent) that reflect an employee's performance on the identified characteristics or dimensions. The formats that are most common, legally defensible, and promising can be classified in two ways: (1) by the type of judgment required, and (2) by the focus of the measure.

First, appraisal systems based on relative judgment ask the supervisor to compare an employee's performance to the performance of other employees doing the same job. Those based on absolute judgments ask the supervisor to make judgments about an employee's performance based solely on performance standards set by the organization. Second, performance measurement systems can be classified by the type of performance data they focus on, such as trait data, behavioral data, or outcome data.

There is no single best appraisal format. Each approach has positives and negatives in terms of administration, development, and legal defensibility. Forms of performance appraisal vary greatly from firm to firm; they can be as simple as periodic one-on-one meetings about performance expectations or be as involved as 360-degree feedback (a system in which feedback is obtained from peers, subordinates, and superiors in order to evaluate performance). As each situation and appraisal system combination presents unique problems, it is important to weigh the positive and negative aspects of the system within your firm. The choice of appraisal system should rest ultimately on the appraisal's primary purpose.

Challenges in Performance Management

How can managers ensure accurate measurement of workers' performance? The primary means is by understanding the barriers that stand in the way. Managers are confronting at least five challenges in this area: (1) rater errors and bias, (2) the influence of affect, (3) organizational politics, (4) individual or group focus, and (5) legal issues.

Rater Errors and Bias

Employees may wonder why it is that certain colleagues receive such outstanding scores when their work performance is measured and suspect that rater errors and bias are to blame. This is a common problem in many organizations. A few of the myriad problems with evaluating performance include employees' access to greater resources, employees' knowledge and ability to "game the system," and halo effects (when an employee is considered to have a lingering "halo," leading him or her to be seen as being a good performer long after a specific positive action or high level of performance was achieved). From time to time, raters simply err in assigning performance levels, and sometimes the system is set up in such a way that it rewards individuals who engage in unethical behavior or figure out how to structure their time at work to earn a particular level of performance evaluation. Regardless of the source of these problems, it is of the greatest importance that systems be designed to reward positive behavior consistent with the organization's mission and goals and to eliminate the possibility of rater error as much as possible. To limit error and bias, perhaps a committee or multiple employees can evaluate the performance of an individual. Another potential option is to have individuals from different locations within the company evaluate employees. Though this is far from an exhaustive list of possibilities, implementing these suggestions certainly would be a step in the right direction.

The Influence of Affect

Study after study has demonstrated that affect, or the degree to which someone likes someone else, significantly influences employee performance appraisal. So, how is it possible to limit this issue? Shouldn't managers have some level of "liking" for their employees? Of course! It is unlikely that affect can be eliminated altogether; however, alternative performance appraisal systems, as discussed earlier, or methods such as 360-degree feedback, which is designed to get multiple inputs, can limit the influence of one individual's like or dislike of another in dictating performance appraisal.

Organizational Politics

Organizations are inherently political, which results in a multitude of problems. However, when organizational politics influence both employee performance and the overall well-being of these employees, problems within a firm can become exacerbated. Eliminating political behavior from your organization, while ideal, is unrealistic. Instead, it is important that the HR function provide oversight for decisions that might be politically motivated and step in to correct them when necessary. By acting as a "checks and balances" system for decisions made by others in the organization, HR is responsible for making sure that these decisions are based on merit, rather than on personal or political connections.

PROBLEM 9-2

Is it appropriate for organizations to evaluate and compensate employees based on objective measures of performance, even though their performance is at least partially determined by factors beyond their control? Should a salesperson, for instance, be paid completely on commission even in the midst of a recession that makes it practically impossible for him or her to sell enough of a product to make a decent living?

SOLUTION

It could be argued that employees should be evaluated and paid only based on performance measures that they are able to control. Another position is that when sales are down, the company is suffering, so it is unreasonable to expect that the company can shield employees from such conditions; in addition, economic downturns might result in layoffs were it not for the commission compensation plans. Whereas salary is a fixed, constant cost that must be paid regardless of changes in company income, commission plans will pay out only when income is realized.

Individual or Group Focus

One question to consider in performance management is whether employees are to be rewarded for their individual performance or for the performance of their group as a whole. This situation can be difficult for those conducting an appraisal. Perhaps an employee is outstanding, but his or her work group's product is subpar. Conversely, a work group might create amazing results, but some of the members may be obviously deficient in their contribution to the effort. While there is no one perfect solution, it is important that teams be rewarded with both the individual and the group in mind. One possibility would be to take multiple components into account in the performance appraisal, including both individual and group factors, and then average them together. Alternatively, if group-focused appraisal is desired, the individuals within the team can help motivate higher levels of performance from everyone involved.

Legal Issues

It is difficult to discuss all of the possible legal issues associated with performance appraisal. There are numerous potential issues dictated by federal or state law designed to protect both employer and employee. It should be noted that if it can be demonstrated that an appraisal was biased, punitive, or unfair, there are specific ramifications outside of the organization, such as monetary damages and other fines and public relations or image impact. For this reason, it is of the utmost importance to ensure that appraisal is applied fairly, evenly, and without bias.

Still Struggling

Errors and bias are some of the most common areas of disagreement between employees and supervisors. Attempts to limit errors and bias can be difficult, but multirater feedback is one of the most effective and easiest to implement solutions. While it is time-consuming, you should consider the benefit of using such a strategy.

Managing Performance

Managing performance is more than periodic reviews of employee performance that result in salary improvements. A complete appraisal process includes informal day-to-day interactions between managers and workers as well as formal face-to-face interviews. Although the ratings themselves are important, what managers do with them is even more critical.

Many managers dread the performance appraisal, particularly if they do not have good news to impart to their employees. In addition, frustration is caused by the fact that most U.S. organizations combine performance appraisals and salary reviews. Because formal appraisal interviews typically are conducted only once a year, they may not always have a substantial and lasting impact on worker performance. However, supervisors who manage performance effectively generally take the following four specific actions:

- They first explore the causes of the performance problem by asking why the problem exists. The manager must understand whether the issue can be attributed to the individual employee or whether the blame lies with the organization. Is the organization providing adequate resources to allow the employee to succeed?

- Once the manager understands the cause of the issue, he or she has to effectively communicate to the employee his or her belief as to why the deficiency exists. It is imperative for the manager to clearly state how he or she intends to work in concert with the employee to solve the problem.

- Third, an action plan must be developed to enable improvement. This plan is sometimes referred to as a *performance plan*. The best way to initiate this action plan is to collaboratively create a list of actionable items that are to be completed on a particular timetable. This can include incremental improvements over time or small, measureable improvements on specific tasks.

- Finally, the manager must provide feedback about the employee's performance and improvements. As with all feedback or appraisal systems, giving timely, specific, and direct feedback about progress and quality will help speed up the process of dealing with subpar performance.

Managers who approach employees from this improvement-based perspective are much more likely to build cohesion within their organization. By focusing on the issues associated with performance and removing the direct blame from the employee (e.g., treating the worker as simply subpar all around), the opportunity to develop the employee is improved. Additionally, when providing direct written feedback to aid performance improvement, the manager gives the employee a road map toward becoming a productive contributor to the organization. Should the employee not meet this set of written expectations, the employer then has documented evidence of the reasons for his or her dismissal, therein limiting the firm's legal liability.

Pay for Performance

Appropriately designed pay-for-performance systems offer managers an excellent opportunity to align employees' interests with the organization's interests. However, pay-for-performance programs are not likely to achieve the desired results unless complementary human resource management (HRM) programs are implemented at the same time. There are a few simple strategies that HR managers can implement to improve the efficacy of pay-for-performance systems:

- *Link pay and performance appropriately.* Make certain that the desired outcomes and rewards are properly linked.
- *Build employee trust.* While this is easier said than done, if employees trust the organization to value them and work in their best interests, the pay-for-performance outcomes will be viewed as legitimate.
- *Demonstrate that performance makes a difference.* Reward those employees that are truly high performers and can act as role models for other employees.
- *Use multiple layers of rewards.* Do not reward just one level of performance (i.e., individual or team), and create different rewards for different levels of performance. This encourages employees at all performance levels to believe that rewards are achievable.
- *Utilize employee involvement.* Seek feedback and input from employees about the design of the pay-for-performance program.
- *Nonfinancial incentives.* It is surprising to many people that nonfinancial incentives can be as effective as or even more effective than financial incentives. Research demonstrates that pay is actually less effective than rewards such as recognition and praise. It is important to match rewards to employee wants and needs as appropriately as possible.

Employees' attitudes about pay are ever-evolving and vary from job to job and from organization to organization. However, there are certain global difficulties when implementing pay-for-performance plans. It is important to consider the following issues in utilizing such plans.

Employees "Doing Only What They Get Paid For"

Many extrinsically motivated employees will do only the "work" that they get paid for. These employees will rarely perform extra-role organizational citizenship behaviors (OCBs). OCBs are actions taken by individual employees for which they receive no direct reward, but instead perform of their own personal volition. Such behavior is considered to help facilitate team building within an organization, but it is not formally required. Examples of OCBs include picking up additional shifts, attending company picnics, or staying after business hours to complete tasks.

Uncooperative Employees

Pay-for-performance plans can encourage unethical or counterproductive behavior at work. It is important to note that if a firm chooses to employ one of these plans that rewards individual performance, the level of cooperation and performance of additional extra-role behaviors may be limited. This lack of extra-role behavior generally comes from employees with a "What's in it for me?" mentality.

Measuring Performance

How exactly will performance be measured and then rewarded? Some jobs lend themselves to piecework-type measurements (e.g., manufacturing jobs), but others are very difficult to quantify, including relationship managers, customer service representatives, and even teachers. For example, how is customer service performance measured? Is it measured via customer satisfaction surveys? Is the measure accurate? Is it biased? Could it be at all possible that someone who provides outstanding customer service might not receive high marks from a particularly dissatisfied customer? In these cases, it is of the greatest importance that measurements of employee performance be multifaceted.

Psychological Contracts

Psychological contracts are agreements between employee and employer that can be spoken or unspoken, but that generally consist of expectations of both the employee and the employer. For example, an employee expects an employer to provide a safe working environment with the proper materials to complete a job efficiently. The employer expects the employee to show up on time and make his or her best effort to do high-quality work while treating coworkers and supervisors with respect. When this "contract" is breached, negative ramifications, such as decreased commitment, lack of performance, and heightened intentions to quit, are the result. If an employer shifts to a pay-for-performance system, there are likely to be psychological contract breach issues with existing employees. An employee who was hired under a different set of expectations may have difficulty adjusting to the new system.

Job Dissatisfaction and Stress

While job dissatisfaction and stress are issues that come up with any performance management system, they are more likely to arise if employees feel unable or unwilling to work under the pay-for-performance system. Such employees may have feelings of entitlement and believe that they should be rewarded based on their perceived value to the company, regardless of their performance. These situations almost always result in decreased performance and increased turnover.

Loss of Intrinsic Drive

What happens when you provide extrinsic rewards for something that people previously did based on intrinsic drive? Motivation theory states that the previous intrinsic drive disappears. In this case, the employer must be prepared to continue extrinsically rewarding the desired behavior. Consider this example: A high school baseball player loves to play the game. This player gets drafted to play professional baseball after his senior year of high school. He goes on to have a fruitful career until one day someone says, "No, we aren't paying you to play anymore." Will he continue to play? Probably not. He has been extrinsically rewarded for something that he initially was intrinsically motivated to do. Once the extrinsic motivation goes away, it is unlikely that he will continue to perform his job function, in this case play baseball professionally.

Types of Pay-for-Performance Plans

Pay-for-performance plans vary in design. They can be designed to reward individuals, teams, business units, the entire organization, or any combination of these.

Individual-Based Plans

Individual-based plans are the most widely used pay-for-performance plans. There are several plans of this type, including merit pay, bonus programs, and awards. Performance that is rewarded under these plans is likely to be repeated. The financial incentives involved can also shape an individual's goals while supporting an individualistic culture. The firm further benefits by achieving individual equity. Disadvantages include the potential promotion of single-mindedness: if employees do not believe that pay and performance are appropriately linked, the programs may work against achieving quality goals and promote inflexibility. In these cases, the firm typically has not clearly stated its expectations and the desired behaviors to be rewarded.

Team-Based Plans

Team-based plans attempt to support efforts to increase the flexibility of the workforce within a firm. These plans normally reward all team members equally based on group outcomes. The advantages of team-based pay-for-performance plans include the fostering of group cohesiveness and the facilitation of performance measurement. Conversely, issues can arise with the team-based plan, including a possible lack of fit with individualistic cultural values and the "free-riding" effect, in which some individuals do not contribute to the group but are rewarded nevertheless. Other disadvantages that can be created relate to social pressures to limit performance, difficulties in identifying meaningful groups, and intergroup competition leading to a decline in overall performance.

Plantwide Plans

These plans reward all workers in a plant or business unit based on the performance of the entire plant or unit. Plantwide plans are generally referred to as gain-sharing programs because they return a portion of the company's cost savings to the workers, usually in the form of a lump-sum bonus. (Three major types of gain-sharing programs are the Scanlon plan, the Rucker plan, and the improshare.) Advantages of these plans include the eliciting of active employee input, an increased level of cooperation, fewer measurement difficulties, and a general improvement in the quality of the product. Disadvantages include the protection of low performers, problems with the criteria used to trigger rewards, and management-labor conflict.

Corporate-Level Plans

Corporate-level plans are the most macro type of incentive program and are based on the entire corporation's performance. The most widely used program of this kind is profit sharing, which differs from gain sharing in three important ways. First, in profit sharing, no attempt is made to reward workers for productivity improvements. Second, the program is very mechanistic, much more so than gain sharing. Third, profit sharing is typically used solely to fund retirement programs.

Employee stock ownership plans (ESOPs) are another type of corporate-wide plan, in which employees are given the opportunity—sometimes at a discounted or favorable rate—to purchase shares of company stock. Advantages of corporatewide plans include financial flexibility for the firm, increased employee commitment, and tax advantages. Disadvantages include risk for employees, limited effect on productivity, and long-run financial difficulties.

Managing performance and appraising employees is truly an art that takes many years and many iterations to master. No two organizations are identical, and it is important to take into account the type of employee, type of work, local labor market, environmental constraints, and competitive dynamics of the market, among other considerations, when approaching performance and appraisal management.

 PROBLEM 9-3

Develop a rating scale for the following jobs: secretary, engineer, and directory assistance operator.

 SOLUTION

Job characteristics may include, but not be limited to, the following: *secretary*—quantity of work, frequency of errors, attendance, and initiative; *engineer*—initiative, significance of contribution to the organization, problem-solving skills, frequency of errors, and communication skills; *directory assistance operator*—speed, attendance, accuracy, and friendliness. In each case, the students should come up with a defining statement that clarifies what each job characteristic means.

Chapter Summary

Performance management and appraisal are two of the most time-consuming facets of the HR function. While these tasks take a significant amount of time, because of their tremendous importance, if you follow the simple tips discussed in this chapter, you can create a user-friendly and highly effective system that both management and employees will find fair and equitable. Designing appraisal process and performance management guidelines that affect all stake-holders (management and line employees) can help build trust in the organiza-tion and limit perceived inequity. If managers communicate freely and openly, employees can understand how and why decisions are made; while they may not like the outcome, if they know the process and believe it to be fair, any negative effect on performance will be minimal.

QUIZ

1. Which of the following is not one of the major types of gain-sharing programs?
   A. Scanlon plan
   B. Rucker plan
   C. Organoshare
   D. Improshare

2. Which of the following is not one of the most common types of employee review?
   A. Self-review
   B. Peer review
   C. Subordinate review
   D. Group review

3. Organizational characteristics that can negatively and positively influence performance are
   A. Performance factors.
   B. Structural factors.
   C. Situational factors.
   D. Simultaneous factors.

4. The identification, measurement, and management of human performance in firms is known as
   A. Employee coaching.
   B. Performance appraisal.
   C. Employee development.
   D. Performance improvement.

5. This is the type of employee appraisal in which supervisors make judgments based on the firm's performance standards.
   A. Supervisor review
   B. Relative judgment
   C. Absolute judgment
   D. Trait appraisal

6. Which of the following is a challenge that may occur when evaluating employee performance?
   A. The influence of affect
   B. Organizational politics
   C. Legal issues
   D. All of the above

7. **This is the type of employee appraisal in which supervisors compare an employee to others who do the same job.**
   A. Supervisor review
   B. Relative judgment
   C. Absolute judgment
   D. Trait appraisal

8. **Which of the following is not a type of pay-for-performance system?**
   A. Individual-based plans
   B. Team-based plans
   C. Plantwide plans
   D. Pair-based plans

9. **Which of the following is not a type of individual-based plan?**
   A. Gain sharing
   B. Merit pay
   C. Bonus programs
   D. Awards

10. **Which of the following is the most common and cost-effective type of pay for sales professionals?**
    A. Straight salary
    B. Flex-pay
    C. Straight commission
    D. A combination plan

chapter 10

Employee Rights and Workplace Safety

This chapter covers the important topics of employee rights, employee responsibilities, and workplace safety. These three topics are key to maintaining a productive workforce and normally are the responsibility of an employee relations specialist. In this chapter, we cover the role of employee relations specialists, their options for employee discipline, and the statutory rights afforded all employees in an organization.

CHAPTER OBJECTIVES

After completing this chapter, the student should be able to

1. Understand the importance of communication in employee relations.
2. Understand and define the value of employee feedback and assistance programs.
3. Identify and understand the statutory rights of employees.

The Roles of the Manager and the Employee Relations Specialist

Although managing employee relations is the responsibility of all managers, effective employee relations requires cooperation between managers and employee relations specialists. Employee relations specialists are members of the HR department who act as internal consultants to the business. They try to ensure that company policies and procedures are followed, and they advise both supervisors and employees on specific employee relations problems. Employee relations policies are designed to provide channels for resolving such problems before they become too serious.

Another role of an employee relations specialist is to prescreen all job applications to help determine the most qualified applicants for open positions within the organization. Employee relations specialists are also responsible for maintaining up-to-date employee records to ensure that the organization is compliant with EEOC requirements. To be an employee relations specialist requires knowledge and experience with human resource management principles, concepts, and practices, as well as knowledge of all federal government policies, regulations, and procedures.

Employee relations specialists may also develop new policies that help maintain fairness and efficiency in the workplace. For example, the client in this situation may be a top manager who is requesting assistance in drafting a new policy on smoking in the workplace or the hiring of employees' spouses.

 PROBLEM 10-1

Some companies attempt to restrict the behavior of employees while they are off the job. The most common restriction is a prohibition of smoking. Less common is a prohibition of public drinking. Is it ethical for a company to try to control its employees' behavior while they are not on the job?

 SOLUTION

Most readers probably believe that companies should not be concerned with what their employees do when they are not at work, or "off the job," unless their actions interfere with their job performance. However, many companies consider one or both of the following factors when making such prohibitions: (1) even when they are not "on duty," employees represent the company in the community, and (2) risky lifestyle behavior is the

company's business, since it will probably have to pay for the results through the employee's health and life insurance benefits. Both employers and employees seem to make valid points in this argument.

Developing Employee Communications

The effectiveness of employee relations management is directly related to the quality of an organization's communications. When supervisors are familiar with the company's employment policies and employees are aware of their rights, there is less opportunity for misunderstandings to arise and productivity to drop. In fact, effective communication among employees creates *higher* productivity, which in turn will increase an organization's bottom line. Another benefit is an increase in loyalty to the company. Organizations will find that after they implement a program for improving communications between employees within the company, the employees experience a much higher sense of engagement with the company and a deep feeling of ownership of the company's objectives. The development and implementation of effective employee communication will prove a vital part of a company's strategy.

As organizations have delegated more responsibility and decision-making authority to employees (who are closer to the customer), the employees' need for access to certain types of related information has increased substantially. Better communication within the company will make it easier for employees to supply consumers with this information.

Types of Information

Two forms of information are sent and received in communications: facts and feelings. *Facts* are pieces of information that can be objectively measured or described. Examples include the cost of a computer, the daily defect rate in a manufacturing plant, and the size of the deductible payment for the company-sponsored health insurance policy. *Feelings* are employees' emotional responses to the decisions made or actions taken by managers or other employees. Examples of these would be an employee being frustrated with his or her boss for taking disciplinary action against a coworker, or an employee verbally attacking a manager over a decision that the manager has made. As pieces of information, facts can be measured even when they are communicated ineffectively. Inappropriately or ineffectively communicating feelings, however, can lead to many problems.

To help avoid potential communication issues, organizations need to design communication channels that allow employees to relay both facts and feelings about specific aspects of their jobs. When organizations open such channels, they build a relationship with their employees and help the entire company create a culture of learning and growth through communication.

How Communication Works

Communication is commonly defined as, "the imparting or interchange of thoughts, opinions, or information by speech, writing, or signs," and it starts with a sender who has a message to give to a receiver. The sender must encode the message and select a communication channel through which to deliver it to the appropriate party. In communicating facts, the message may be encoded as words, numbers, or digital symbols; in communicating feelings, it may be encoded as body language or tone of voice. The requirement of the action of communication is that everyone involved has an area of communicative commonality.

Communications that provide for feedback are called *two-way* communications because they allow the sender and the receiver to interact with each other. Examples of two-way communication are talking on the phone, instant messaging on your computer, using networks of computers, and having a discussion between two people in person. Communications that provide no opportunity for feedback are called *one-way* communications. An example of a one-way communication is the establishment of an organization's rules, regulations, and procedures that are passed down to its employees.

Downward and Upward Communication

Employee relations specialists help maintain both *downward* communication and *upward* communication in an organization. Downward communication, in which management passes information "down" to employees, allows managers to implement the decisions that they have made and to influence employees who are lower in the organizational hierarchy. By creating effective downward communication, organizations increase their efficiency and productivity.

Employee morale and loyalty are also increased by ensuring that all employees are on board with the company's objectives.

Upward communication, in which employees pass information "up" to management, allows employees at lower levels of the organization to communicate their ideas or feelings to higher-level decision makers. Upward communication is an important tool that many organizations do not necessarily use. When it is used, however, the thoughts and ideas of an organization's employees can contribute to the company's progress and help it surpass its competitors. Employees who are given the option of upward communication exhibit more pride in their work and experience a stronger sense of ownership within the company. Furthermore, employees' motivation levels will increase as they feel more valued and respected by their organization.

Formal and Informal Communication

Formal communication occurs through designated official organizational channels. For example, a company's employee relations specialist will hold official meetings or issue letters and memos throughout the firm. *Informal* communication is any communication done outside of official organizational channels or networks. Examples of this type include gossiping at the watercooler, chatting over lunch, or casual encounters in the hallway. Informal communication can be good, since it helps to improve working relationships and generate ideas within the company in a relaxed environment. A downside of such casual communication is that it can assist in the spreading of rumors and misconstrued facts. With the help of formal communication from the top down, however, employees will continue to understand the company's objectives, regardless of any misconstrued rumors.

Internal and External Communications

Among the many responsibilities of an organization's employee relations specialist, both communication within the organization and communication about the organization to its community and external environment are imperative. An organization's *internal* communication is shown in many different ways, including company and team briefings, notices, company reports, memos, and internal e-mails. *External* communication consists of communication through the company's Web site, direct mail, organizational advertising, and job postings for future applicants.

Still Struggling

Communication is perhaps the most important function of human resources. If an employee relations specialist is not an effective communicator, his or her job will prove to be incredibly difficult. Electronic communication, while cost-effective and convenient, can sometimes hinder effective communication. Before "firing off an e-mail" about a potentially sensitive subject, consider the potential ramifications. In most cases, traditional face-to-face communication is the best method to ensure clarity and understanding of the message.

Encouraging Effective Communication

Working with supervisors and managers, employee relations representatives can facilitate effective communication by developing and maintaining four types of programs: (1) information dissemination programs, (2) employee feedback programs, (3) employee assistance programs, and (4) employee recognition programs.

Information Dissemination Programs

Information dissemination involves making information available to decision makers, wherever they are located. The employee handbook is probably the most important source of information that the HR department can provide, and it sets the tone for the company's overall employee relations philosophy. There are many other forms of written communication besides the employee handbook that can be used to alert employees of important information, including memos and newsletters.

The Employee Handbook

The employee handbook provides detailed guidelines concerning an organization's expectations and procedures. An organization's employee relations specialist is responsible for effectively distributing the handbook to all new hires at the beginning of their training in an effort to help new employees become accustomed to the company and its policies and procedures. Employee handbooks may include:

- *A welcome statement, along with a brief description of the company's successful history and how an employee can contribute to the organization's continued success.* A mission statement and/or statements about the goals and objectives of the company are also likely to be included.

- *Orientation procedures that outline the required government forms, proof of identity, and eligibility for employment documents that the new employee must submit.* The requirement of a successfully completed drug test as well as other forms may be included.

- *Definitions of full- and part-time employment and the benefits that employees in each classification receive.* In addition, information about breaks and lunch may be provided here.

- *Employee compensation.* This section will also outline policies concerning vacation and insurance pay, benefits, the 401(k), retirement, and raises.

- *Guidelines for employees when they are up for performance reviews.* This will state when and how the reviews will be conducted.

- *The organization's expectations about conduct and its disciplinary policies.* Sexual harassment, alcohol and drug use, and attendance may be discussed here.

- *A company's grounds for dismissal and due process.*

- *Rules concerning mail, use of cell phone or telephone while working, company equipment, surfing the Web for personal use, and the use of company vehicles for job assignments.*

- *An employee's voluntary withdrawal of employment and exit interviews.*

- *Company requirements with regard to private information and the employee's responsibility concerning this confidential information.* This information may include the release of employee records, along with an explanation of who is allowed to view this information.

Written Communications

Written communications include memos, financial statements, newsletters, and bulletins that are viewed by the employees. Written communication gives power to the receiver.

Because of people's ability to forget or confuse information, written communication provides a cost-effective and permanent reviewable record. Often, this written material may be drafted numerous times to ensure that the information is presented in the most effective and accurate manner.

Audiovisual Communications

Audiovisual communications are a creative and powerful way to engage your audience, whether it be your employees, your customers, the public, or the media. For example, themed videos on specific aspects of the organization, such as safety, may be presented to employees. Orientation for new hires typically involves some type of audiovisual communication as well. In general, the use of audiovisual materials can be an effective way to get a direct message to the receiver while attempting to avoid lost, confused, or misinterpreted information, which is more prevalent in other forms of communication.

Electronic Communications

New technologies have made it possible to disseminate information beyond the printed word, using visual images and audio as powerful communication tools. Teleconferencing, for example, allows people with busy schedules to participate in meetings even when they are a great distance away from the conference location (or each other). Advances in electronic communications (voice mail and e-mail) have made interactive communication between sender and receiver possible even when they are separated by physical distance and busy schedules. Electronic communication has increased the ease of sending and receiving information and, therefore, the overall success of organizations.

Electronic Mail (E-mail)

E-mail is perhaps the most common form of communication in organizations today. Typically, it is used for the transfer of data, images, signals, and signs, and it can also be used for communication with people who are hearing impaired. This form of almost instantaneous communication is inexpensive and can be used at the sender's and the receiver's convenience. For this reason, the days of the hard-copy corporate memo are gone. By allowing passive communication among employees from multiple levels of the organization, e-mail has become the cornerstone of today's corporate communication structure.

 PROBLEM 10-2

Should companies have the right to read and monitor their employees' e-mail?

 SOLUTION

Most people believe that companies should not have the right to read and monitor employees' e-mail. However, keep in mind that the whole system that an employee operates at work is the company's property. The company

provides the technology infrastructure that enables e-mail access, and employees are compensated for their time at work. If employees want to send personal e-mail, they should use their own system and service provider, not the one given to them at work.

Meetings

Formal meetings are opportunities for face-to-face communication between two or more employees and are guided by a specific agenda. These meetings facilitate dialogue and promote the nurturing of personal relationships, particularly among employees who may not interact frequently because they are separated by organizational or geographic barriers.

Retreats

Retreats provide both a great way to bring employees together and a reward to employees for their work. They help strengthen the bonds among coworkers that already exist, while also creating new ones. Retreats are another way to increase employee loyalty by showing workers that they are valued and that hard work pays off. Such situations can also present an opportunity to train employees effectively on ways to perform better.

Informal Communication

Informal communication in the workplace satisfies the needs of employees through social interactions and the expression of emotional feelings. This communication is not based on a person's standing in the hierarchy of the organization, although sometimes an employee's position in the organization can interrupt or deny this informal communication. Informal communication is much more relaxed and casual than most other forms of communication within the workplace. Information discussed informally is typically done by word of mouth and can spread rapidly throughout the organization, with no restrictions. Some examples of informal communication include the aforementioned water-cooler gossip, overheard conversations between other employees, "hallway talk," or information, whether true or not, that is spread during random or casual encounters with colleagues.

Departmental Offices

Departmental offices are locations within the organization where members of a department can perform tasks and discuss plans and ideas for the future in either a formal or an informal manner. In this setting, coworkers have the opportunity to provide input and discuss their current work and focuses.

Employee Feedback Programs

To provide upward communication channels between employees and management, many organizations offer employee feedback programs. These programs are designed to improve management-employee relations by giving employees a voice in decision making and policy formulation, while making sure that they receive due process on any complaints that they lodge against managers. The most common employee feedback programs are employee attitude surveys and appeals procedures.

Employee Attitude Surveys

The organization's needs are depicted in employee attitude surveys. The surveys are used by the organization to gather employees' opinions and knowledge on issues that the company may be facing. If the company is to communicate effectively with its employees, it is important for it to involve the employees in these surveys.

Appeals Procedures

Sometimes employees have issues with their coworkers or managers. When this happens, it is important for an organization to provide an environment in which these employees can communicate their issues and grievances to a manager in an effort to resolve the situation. Appeals procedures provide such an environment. This is a way for organizations to show their employees that they care about how the employees are treated and to retain information on how to continually improve their relationships with their employees and those employees' morale. In the event that these procedures do not resolve the dispute, there are other steps that can be taken. For example, the employee may file a grievance through a filing procedure with the appointing authority (this process should be clearly set forth in an employee handbook or other orientation materials).

Employee Assistance Programs

Employee assistance programs (EAPs) help employees cope with personal problems (physical, mental, or emotional) that are interfering with their job performance. These problems may include alcohol or drug abuse, domestic violence, elder care, AIDS and other diseases, eating disorders, and compulsive gambling. Assessments, counseling, or referral services for employees, and also for others in their household, can be provided through an EAP. These types of programs are usually paid for by an employer and free to the employees. Confidentiality is an important component of these programs and should be maintained in accordance with privacy laws and professional ethical standards. Employee assistance programs benefit the organization by lowering medical costs, reducing turnover and absenteeism, and creating higher employee productivity and morale.

Employee Recognition Programs

Employee recognition programs enhance effective employee relations by communicating that the organization cares about employees' ideas and is willing to reward them for their efforts. These programs help build a culture of teamwork through recognition and respect, with employees that are on board with their organizations' objectives.

A recognition system is a network of strategically linked recognition programs that acknowledges measurable work and reinforces performance standards. This type of recognition can improve an employee's morale, which in turn helps to increase his or her productivity. It can also help in reducing employee turnover and absenteeism by creating an environment that employees want to contribute to. The HR department can help facilitate this recognition system by developing and maintaining formal employee recognition programs, such as recognition awards and rewards, and suggestion systems.

Recognition Awards and Rewards

Recognition awards give public credit to people or teams that make outstanding contributions to the organization. Rewards do not always have to be in the form of money. Great examples of alternative ways to reward employees could be having the boss wash the employee's car in front of others, or having managers serve the employee's lunch. These programs assist in creating more value of sorts for the employees and, in turn, create a greater sense of cohesion among employees.

Suggestion Systems

Suggestion systems are designed to solicit, evaluate, and implement suggestions from employees, and then reward the employees for worthwhile ideas. Employees bring great ideas to an organization, and it is important for companies to use this input to help them resolve issues dealing with cost savings, product quality, workplace efficiency, customer service, and working conditions.

Suggestion systems may be as simple as a box located in a general area of the organization or a much more formal process in which a committee reviews ideas and rewards the employees responsible for those that are implemented. An idea can suggest improvements that are both simple and easy or can solve a big issue for a company. An example of a simple improvement could be putting a refrigerator in the coffee room, or on a larger scale, you could save the company thousands of dollars a year by switching all employees' company cell phones to a group contract with a discount vendor.

By recognizing its employees through recognition awards and suggestion systems, an organization builds greater bonds with those employees. In turn, companies may find an increase in customer loyalty and retention as a result of better service, better products, or a better general experience interacting with employees, potentially strengthening the company's brand image both externally and internally.

PROBLEM 10-3

Why do employees in some companies not take suggestion systems seriously? What can management do to improve the credibility of its employee suggestion system?

 SOLUTION

In some companies, the suggestion system may not be seen as being fair in how it determines awards, or it may be viewed as a facade, with suggestions not being taken seriously. One thing that could be done to improve the program's credibility is to use a committee of employees to evaluate each suggestion. The significance and visibility of the recognition award will create further credibility. Finally, the process of implementing suggestions should not take so long as to make the suggestions lose their importance.

Employee Rights

Employees' rights allow them to engage in conduct that is protected by federal and state laws and social sanctions. These laws provide employees with specific protection in their relationship with their employer, including protection from wrongful discharge. The rights include statutory, contractual, and other basic human rights.

Statutory Rights

Statutory rights are those rights that are afforded to individuals by law. The key statutory rights can be found in laws such as Title VII of the Civil Rights Act (1964), the Occupational Safety and Health Act (OSHA), and the National Labor Relations Act (NLRA). The rights that employees have under these laws include statutory sick pay, maternity pay and leave, and compensation accrued toward their state pension and unemployment benefits. Oftentimes an employee is entitled to paid leave annually and to redundancy pay. Redundancy pay is usually a sum of money, based on factors such as hours worked and duration with the company, given to an employee who is being laid off from the organization.

Contractual Rights

Contractual rights are entitlements that have been agreed upon between two parties, either verbally or in writing. A written employment contract details the terms of the employment relationship. These contracts usually address such issues as seniority, due process, and wrongful discharge. In addition to written contracts, there are implied contracts. Employee handbooks, employment policies, and statements made by an interviewer or manager may be interpreted by the courts as creating an implied contract. An implied contract is legally enforceable and arises when two parties knowingly accept terms that benefit them.

Other Basic Human Rights

Beyond statutory and contract rights, employees may have rights to ethical treatment, in that they should be treated without bias and in a manner consistent with professional ethical standards; limited free speech, as they should not feel that they are being "censored" by their employers; and limited privacy, as certain aspects of their day-to-day work life should not be subject to public scrutiny.

Management Rights

Management rights are the rights of managers to run the business and to retain any profits generated. In particular, these rights include the right to direct and lead the workforce (e.g., to hire employees and set pay levels). Often, these rights are residual, meaning that they are not affected by contracts or other laws (e.g., EEO-related).

Employment at Will

The employment-at-will rule was adopted by the U.S. courts in the nineteenth century. Workers were free to terminate their relationship (employment) for any reason, so the courts deemed it fair for employers to be able to do the same. This rule has stacked the deck in favor of employers, giving wrongfully discharged employees little legal recourse. Organizations can terminate employees based on any criteria that they deem appropriate, regardless of the employees' or others' opinions. Nevertheless, employment at will is limited in certain situations, such as an employer terminating an employee for reasons that amount to discrimination. Other limitations include cases of public policy exception, implied contracts, and lack of good faith and fair dealing.

The public policy exception prevents organizations from wrongfully discharging an employee when doing so would violate rules that have been explicitly established by the state. Examples of this situation would be the firing of an employee when he or she filed for workers' compensation after an on-the-job injury or firing an employee for not participating in an illegal activity that was condoned by an employer.

 PROBLEM 10-4

Is it ethical to require all employees to sign an employment-at-will statement acknowledging that they understand that the employer can terminate their employment at any time for any reason?

 SOLUTION

Since many employers have this right, it could be considered a strong ethical move to clearly inform employees of their employment rights, rather than surprise them if the need for termination arises.

The implied contract exception states that even though there may be only an implied contract, when representations or agreements have been made by an organization, these representations or agreements are sometimes considered just as valid as a written, signed, and executed contract. In such a case, a firm can be subject to contract law even if there is no written agreement with the employee. For example, if an employee handbook includes information on employees' rights with regard to the procedure for termination, it is implied that the employer will follow that specific procedure. Another example would be that when members of an organization verbally communicate to employees that their employment will continue as long as their performance is appropriate, then the organization may terminate those employees only with just cause.

The good faith and fair dealing exception basically says that organizations and their representatives may not terminate an employee out of malice or in bad faith. For example, a firm should not terminate an employee because he or she disagrees philosophically with a member of the management team, nor should it terminate an employee simply to "send a message" to other employees about acceptable behavior.

Still Struggling

Employment at will can be a difficult right for management to exercise. Regardless of employers' ability to dismiss employees at any time for any reason, it is in the company's best interests to enact a progressive discipline policy and document any employee issues properly in case the employer is ever challenged about the fairness of an employee's subsequent termination.

Employee Rights Challenges: A Balancing Act

There is a thin line between the rights of employees and the rights of management. Workplace issues such as random drug testing, electronic monitoring, and whistle-blowing highlight the conflict between the two.

Random Drug Testing

The Drug-Free Workplace Act was enacted in 1988. Companies that use drug tests must address several challenges, including the establishment of a policy, what to do about false positives, how to ensure the security of urine specimens, and whether alternative tests should be used (e.g., performance tests). Although it is important for organizations to protect their other workers and consumers from employees who are working under the influence, many legal professionals consider random drug testing to be an invasion of personal privacy and an unreasonable search and, potentially, seizure process.

Electronic Monitoring

Companies attempt to fight various forms of employee theft by electronic monitoring. If companies are to use this type of monitoring successfully, the employees should know what devices are being utilized, the employer should create ways in which monitoring is beneficial to the employees, and the employer should develop appropriate policies that are publicized throughout the company. Examples of electronic monitoring include

- Telephone monitoring
- Computer monitoring
- Electronic mail and voice mail monitoring
- Video monitoring

Whistle-blowing

A whistle-blower is a person, typically within the company, who raises a concern about wrongdoing that is taking place in an organization. This wrongdoing can include violations of a law, rule, or regulation, or a direct threat to the public interest, such as fraud, health and safety violations, and corruption.

Whistle-blowers can come forward with evidence of the issue either internally or externally. Internally, the employee would speak with others within the organization. Externally, the employee would speak with regulators, law enforcement agencies, the media, or other groups with a concern about the illegal or unethical activity. While federal employees who are whistle-blowers have certain legal protections, private-sector employees do not. Because employees may decide to blow the whistle on their employer, many companies realize that it is in their best interest to establish a policy on whistle-blowing. As a result, whistle-blowers will often face reprisals from the organization itself, related organizations, or even the law. Federal legislation has been enacted to help protect whistle-blowers from retaliation. Most recently, the Sarbanes-Oxley Act of 2002 sets out criminal penalties for retaliation against whistle-blowers.

Workplace Safety and the Law

All levels of government have passed numerous laws to regulate workplace safety. Many of these laws include detailed regulations dealing with hazards in specific industries, such as coal mining and railroads, but many of them also relate to general safety and health conditions.

Typically each state will have its own program to enforce health and safety issues that are of particular interest to citizens of that state. The jurisdictions of state programs include all private- and public-sector employers and employees throughout the state, with the exception of maritime industries. These state programs must maintain standards that are "at least as effective" as comparable federal standards. States generally set up enforcement programs, voluntary and cooperative programs, informal conferences and appeals, and basic policies and procedures.

Occupational Safety and Health Administration

The primary federal laws governing workplace safety are administered by the Occupational Safety and Health Administration (OSHA). OSHA is an agency of the U.S. Department of Labor whose mission is to prevent work-related injuries, illnesses, and occupational fatalities by issuing and enforcing standards for workplace safety and health. The agency is headed by a deputy assistant secretary of labor.

To ensure the safety and health of workers in the United States, OSHA works with employers and employees to create better working environments. One of OSHA's principal duties is to be active in workplace inspections to ensure compliance with governmental standards and laws. Consultation programs and technical assistance from OSHA help to ensure that these safety standards are being met. Both OSHA and workers' compensation laws affect most workers, but OSHA does not *provide* compensation for workers.

The Occupational Safety and Health Act

OSHA was created by Congress under the Occupational Safety and Health Act (OSH Act), signed by President Richard M. Nixon on December 29, 1970. The act assigns to OSHA the duties of setting safety standards and conducting inspections to ensure that employers are providing safe and healthful workplaces.

The act imposes three major obligations on employers: (1) to provide a safe and healthy work environment, (2) to comply with specific occupational safety and health standards, and (3) to keep records of occupational injuries and illnesses. The Occupational Safety and Health Administration has the primary responsibility for enforcing the OSH Act.

The OSH Act also created the National Institute for Occupational Safety and Health (NIOSH) as a research agency focusing on occupational health and safety.

The National Institute for Occupational Safety and Health

The National Institute for Occupational Safety and Health is the U.S. federal agency that is responsible for conducting research and making recommendations for the prevention of work-related injury and illness. Unlike OSHA, which is part of the U.S. Department of Labor), NIOSH is part of the Centers for Disease Control and Prevention (CDC) within the U.S. Department of Health and Human Services.

The Occupational Safety and Health Review Commission (OSHRC)

In addition to OSHA and NIOSH, the Occupational Safety and Health Review Commission (OSHRC) is an independent federal agency that was created under the Occupational Safety and Health Act of 1970. The commission has the task of deciding the citations or penalties resulting from OSHA inspections of American workplaces.

Managing Contemporary Safety, Health, and Behavioral Issues

Managers must deal with a variety of practical, legal, and ethical issues, many of which involve balancing individual rights against organizational needs. Because these issues often give rise to legal and ethical issues, HRM professionals are frequently called upon to develop and implement policies to deal with them. Here, we examine some of the weightiest issues facing employers today.

AIDS and Other Chronic Illnesses

Dealing effectively with workplace concerns that arise when an employee contracts AIDS or some other chronic illness is one of the most important workplace health challenges today. Organizations can develop internal policies and procedures when they are placed in a situation in which this issue comes into play. When these policies are developed, they should be properly communicated throughout the organization so that everyone in the company can express his or her opinions and points of view on ways to improve the policy, and so that the company can encourage all employees to be on board with it. In addition, it is important to realize that persons with HIV, both symptomatic and asymptomatic, have physical impairments that substantially limit one or more major life activities and thus are protected by the Americans with Disabilities Act.

The American with Disabilities Act and the Manager's Role

The Americans with Disabilities Act (ADA) gives to individuals with disabilities federal civil rights protection similar to the rights provided to individuals on the basis of race, color, sex, national origin, age, and religion. The act guarantees equal opportunity for individuals with disabilities in public accommodations, employment, transportation, state and local government services, and telecommunications. An individual is considered to have a "disability" if he or she has a physical or mental impairment that substantially limits one or more major life activities, has a record of such an impairment, or is regarded as having such an impairment.

Violence in the Workplace

In addition to the accommodations provided to disabled employees and protection from job-related dangers (via OSHA), firms must also prepare for the possibility of physical harm coming to their employees as a result of acts of violence. While everyone hopes that preparations for dealing with potentially violent situations are never needed, your firm is better served by being safe rather than sorry when it comes to dealing with violence at work.

Statistics show that the number of homicides at work is declining, but scenarios of workplace homicide are still too common. According to the U.S. Department of Labor, homicide is second only to highway fatalities in causing death at work. This being the case, it is important to follow these guidelines to reduce potential assaults and threats and to create a safe, productive environment in which an employee's rights, and his or her personal being, are protected.

- *When hiring employees, be diligent about background checks.* At the same time, be careful not to violate employees' privacy or include impermissible questions in the interview.
- *Assess vulnerabilities on a regular basis.* Starting places for security audits include workers' compensation records, employee disciplinary files, OSHA reports, security reports, and personnel files.
- *Implement violence prevention policies.* Organizations should have violence prevention policies in place while providing confidentiality and support for victims of violence in the workplace.

- *Conduct training on violence and workplace safety regularly.* Everyone in the organization should be aware of where the company stands with regard to workplace violence as well as what employees should do if they experience it. There should also be additional training for upper management on threat management and security implementation.

- *When terminating an employee, do it respectfully.* Termination of an employee is a sensitive issue and carries the potential for a violent reaction if it is not handled delicately.

- *Organizations should have a weapons ban.* A May 2005 study published in the *American Journal of Public Health* found that workplaces in which guns were permitted were five to seven times more likely to be the site of a workplace homicide than those where they were not.

Smoking in the Workplace

The push to restrict workplace smoking has come largely in the last decade. Smoke-free workplaces are rapidly becoming the norm in the United States.

Employees benefit from a smoke-free workplace in a number of ways. A smoking ban contributes to the creation of a safe and healthy environment. If an organization is able to implement a ban successfully, it shows its employees that it cares about their health and is taking proactive steps to improve it. On the most basic level, employees who are bothered by smoke will no longer have to deal with the issue. Of course, it is imperative that the company is clear on the subject so that all employees understand the policy. Nonsmokers and smokers alike will appreciate such clarity.

Employers also benefit from a smoke-free workplace, starting most fundamentally with providing an environment that is safe and healthy for all employees. Furthermore, direct health-care costs may be reduced as employees are indirectly encouraged not to smoke. A decrease in maintenance costs for the cleanup related to smoking may also occur. Finally, it may be possible for the organization to negotiate the cost of its insurance coverage down when employee smoking is reduced.

Cumulative Trauma Disorders

Cumulative trauma disorders (CTDs) refers to a wide range of maladies ranging from carpal tunnel syndrome to tennis elbow. CTDs are also called repetitive stress (or motion or strain) injuries (or illnesses or syndromes). The number of workers with CTDs has risen dramatically in recent years. This growth is of concern to large and small manufacturers, insurance carriers, health-care providers, and government agencies.

Safety and Health Programs

To cope with physical hazards and other hazards such as stress, unsafe behavior, and poor health habits, employers often design comprehensive safety and health programs. Among these are safety programs and wellness programs.

Safety Programs

A safe working environment does not just happen; it has to be created. The organizations with the best reputations for safety have developed well-planned and thorough safety programs. It is important that you evaluate your company's needs and develop a safety program based on those needs, keeping in mind any potential hazards that your organization may face. Once you have established this program, the entire organization needs to follow through with it. If you have trouble implementing the program companywide, you may seek assistance from your state consultation program.

Once your program is in effect, you will be able to identify conditions or situations where illness or injury could occur and prevent it from happening.

Wellness Programs

As health-care costs have skyrocketed over the last two decades, organizations have become more interested in preventive programs. Good health and exercise affect more than just our physical well-being—they benefit our state of mind, increase productivity, enhance self-esteem, and more. May is a month for recognizing and encouraging health and well-being, both physically and mentally, and it is a good time to start implementing a wellness program if your company has not already done so.

Chapter Summary

It is crucial to keep in mind the full set of rights that are afforded to employees at work. A feeling of indentured servitude will no longer suffice to retain valued employees. In today's global marketplace, employees are free to move from firm to firm almost seamlessly. Understanding the rights of employees and their value is the cornerstone of valuing the contributions of your employees. When an individual feels valued and is allowed to complete his or her assigned work without interference, that individual will generally provide his or her employer with high-quality outputs. In addition, safety at work is a universal right that is usually overlooked until a problem arises. While it is the responsibility of both the employee and the employer to maintain a safe and productive workplace, HR should make every effort to ensure employee safety.

QUIZ

1. Electronic monitoring
   A. Is required by law.
   B. Must be disclosed to employees.
   C. Is not effective.
   D. Is the right of every employer.

2. The two forms of information that are sent and received in communications are
   A. Facts and feelings.
   B. Personal and public.
   C. Implied and overt.
   D. Experienced and expressed.

3. This form of communication allows managers to implement the decisions they have made and to influence employees who are lower in the organizational hierarchy.
   A. Upward
   B. Downward
   C. Organizational
   D. Divisional

4. Drug testing
   A. Should be conducted by every organization, regardless of the type of work that is being done.
   B. Has many stipulations associated with it that must be followed and communicated.
   C. Is necessary only for dangerous jobs.
   D. Has a high cost and few benefits.

5. At-will employment
   A. States that employees can be fired at any time for any reason.
   B. Provides legal recourse for the employee.
   C. Allows private companies to discriminate based on race and gender.
   D. Both a and b.

6. Employee assistance programs (EAPs) typically deal with which of the following?
   A. Alcohol and/or alcohol abuse
   B. Compulsive gambling
   C. Eating disorders
   D. All of the above

7. **What act includes protection against retaliation against whistle-blowers?**
   A. Equal Rights Amendment of 1972
   B. Sarbanes-Oxley Act of 2002
   C. Fair Labor Standards Act of 1938
   D. Executive Order 11246

8. **Employee recognition systems**
   A. Enhance employee performance and commitment.
   B. Are costly and rarely produce results.
   C. Give only short-term rewards.
   D. Are highly political in nature.

9. **What is the most cost-effective and efficient form of organizational communication?**
   A. Memos
   B. Telephone communication
   C. Face-to-face communication
   D. Electronic mail communication

10. **HR managers have a responsibility to communicate effectively with employees because**
    A. They are advocates for employees and can provide services for them.
    B. They are the primary point of contact for employee relations issues.
    C. Both A and B.
    D. None of the above.

chapter **11**

Employee Discipline and Responsibilities

Just as employees are given certain rights, discussed in the previous chapter, they also have a number of responsibilities, regardless of their place of work. Should an employee not meet the responsibilities of his or her position, an HR manager needs to understand how to effectively and developmentally discipline that employee. This chapter seeks to explain the sometimes esoteric worlds of employee discipline and responsibilities.

CHAPTER OBJECTIVES

After completing this chapter, the student should be able to

1. Identify the legal responsibilities of employees at work.

2. Understand the process of progressive discipline.

3. Describe options for developmentally providing corrective discipline to employees.

Disciplining Employees

Employee discipline is a tool that managers use to communicate to an employee a need to change his or her behavior. Traditionally, such discipline has been performed by supervisors. Today, the responsibility for disciplining an employee may lie with a team of the employee's peers, a review panel, multiple consulting managers, or other members of the organization. There are two different approaches to discipline that are widely used: (1) progressive discipline and (2) positive discipline.

Progressive Discipline

The most commonly used form of discipline, progressive discipline, consists of a series of management interventions that gives employees opportunities to correct their behavior before being discharged. This approach results in a graduated range of discipline, from mild to severe, to respond to an employee's misconduct or lack of performance. It is imperative for the health of the organization that the system always responds appropriately and in proportion to the employees' behavior.

Progressive discipline should begin with the supervisor or manager speaking with the employee privately to communicate the issue. This initial step gives the employee the chance to understand where improvement is needed and the efforts that the manager will make to assist the employee in the process. If the behavior or lack of performance continues, a formal written warning should be created and given to the employee. This document should describe the areas of concern and should be signed by both the employee and his or her supervisor or manager. The document should be clear and concise and should be placed with the employee's records in Human Resources. If the issue of concern continues, depending on how severe it is, you may decide either to terminate the employee or to issue another formal written document. If you issue another warning, it should state that this is the last chance for the change in behavior or performance requirements. The last warning or termination of an employee should be done in the presence of another person, such as a human resources officer.

Positive Discipline

Encouraging employees to monitor their own behaviors and assume responsibility for their own actions is called *positive discipline*. Management still intervenes, but with counseling sessions as opposed to punishment. Creating an atmosphere of positive discipline builds trust and a greater understanding of the organization's expectations. For this system to succeed, employees must make a concerted effort in their self-discipline, and the organization must set clear, obtainable, and well-communicated rules. Business, just like life, is not always black and white, and problematic situations are bound to arise. However, as long as there is effective communication among all the parties involved, it should be possible to resolve these issues.

Administering and Managing Discipline

Managers must make sure that employees who are disciplined receive due process, ensure that all evidence and points of view are considered, and see that employees receive fair and consistent treatment, meaning that each employee is treated in the same manner regardless of his or her rank, tenure, or political savvy.

Supervisors should be properly trained in how to administer discipline and how to address two important elements of due process: (1) the standards of discipline and (2) the employee's right to appeal a disciplinary action. If supervisors are not properly trained on how to handle disciplinary actions, the result could be litigation.

 PROBLEM 11-1

What are the advantages and disadvantages of letting a team administer discipline to one of its members?

 SOLUTION

There can be many advantages to allowing teams to administer discipline to their own members. First, if they are properly trained, team members will often be more demanding than managers. Second, they are more likely to know what performance issues actually exist and are more likely to be fair in executing disciplinary action. Third, the discipline will have the support of the employees within the team, creating better team morale overall.

Disadvantages of this process include the difficulty for employees of disciplining their friends, peers, or coworkers who are at the same level as themselves, which could result in a great amount of tension within the team. Second, without training, disciplinary actions enacted by team members may be inconsistent. Third, team members may resent management's "passing the buck" to them, especially if they believe that the administration of discipline should lie solely with managers or supervisors.

Basic Standards of Discipline

There are three basic standards of discipline for all rule violations: (1) communication of criteria, (2) documentation of facts, and (3) consistent responses to infractions.

The Just Cause Standard of Discipline

The requirement of just cause protects employees from arbitrary or unfair termination, as well as from other forms of inappropriate discipline. Just cause has become a standard in labor arbitration and has been included in many labor contracts as a source of job security. In arbitration, when an employer is proposing termination, suspension, or some other form of discipline, it must prove that the employee has committed a violation of a company policy or rule. In many wrongful discharge cases, the U.S. courts place the burden of proof squarely on the employer, and the applicable standard (just cause) is stringent. Just cause is therefore a burden of proof or standard that an employer must meet in order to justify discipline or discharge. Because of this, employers who believe that their employees work under employment at will (discussed in the previous chapter) may decide on a less demanding standard.

The Right to Appeal Discipline

For a discipline system to be effective, employees must have access to an appeal procedure so that those who believe that they have been wrongly disciplined are able to challenge a disciplinary decision made by management. Two of the most useful appeals procedures are the open-door policy and the use of employee relations representatives (grievance procedure).

An open-door policy is one in which an employee may speak openly with any manager in the organization, including the CEO, about an issue that he or she feels needs to be dealt with. This policy helps the employee navigate the chain of command and politics within an organization so that the issue that the employee is raising can be handled appropriately and efficiently. Similarly, employee relations representatives help employees bring disciplinary or other job-related concerns to the attention of management. The open-door policy and a grievance procedure are effective tools in an employee's appeal.

Managing Difficult Employees

Managing the discipline of difficult employees requires good judgment and common sense. It also requires that the organization have clear, easy-to-follow rules that everyone understands and that all employees can abide by.

Issues that may arise in dealing with difficult employees include poor attendance, poor performance, insubordination, and substance abuse. The following steps must be taken to identify and take the necessary actions in disciplining a difficult employee:

- Look at the situation from both sides.
- Examine the facts of the situation.
- Determine the best strategy for handling the situation.
- Confront the employee and discuss the situation with him or her.
- Take appropriate action to deal with the behavior displayed by the employee.

 PROBLEM 11-2

You discover that your superior has been billing the company for business trips that she never took. When you ask her about it, she says that this is common practice throughout the company, the other department heads do the same thing, and corporate headquarters has set reimbursement rates so low that employees have to pad their expense accounts if they are to be fairly reimbursed. What should you do?

 SOLUTION

There are a wide variety of responses to this question. If, in fact, the practice is widespread, reporting it may be futile because the officials you contact may be engaging in the same actions. However, as some people point out, just because a number of managers or employees are involved doesn't make the practice ethical. Additionally, the practice may not be as widespread as your boss is leading you to believe. Another aspect to consider is whether there is a whistle-blowing policy within your company that will protect you from disciplinary actions such as termination in such a situation. If not, you may lose your job by reporting one of your superiors. The ethical question then becomes, is this offense serious enough for you to risk losing your job?

Poor Attendance

Absenteeism and tardiness are included in the problem of poor attendance and are considered serious charges that could lead to termination. When employees put themselves and their supervisors in a position where discipline needs to be administered because of poor attendance, it is imperative to hold the employees accountable for their behavior. Supervisors and managers need to stay on top of attendance problems from the beginning. Greater issues could occur if managers wait until the problem grows and find that absent or tardy employees claim that they did not know that their attendance was a problem, since nothing was ever said to them. A manager or supervisor needs to maintain a certain level of strictness, depending on the company, so that employees realize that their job starts at a specific time, and that if they are not able to meet such a requirement, then something must be done.

In disciplining an employee for poor attendance, managers need to consider three main factors. First, is the attendance rule set by the company a reasonable one? If not, there may be some leeway in disciplinary action, or if many employees are having trouble meeting the standard, managers may need to consider alternative rules. Second, has the employee been warned of the consequences of poor attendance? If the answer is no, then the managers must implement a system to make sure that all employees are aware of the company's policies concerning poor attendance. If it is yes, then any claim of ignorance on the employee's part would be invalid and disciplinary steps should be taken. Third, are there any mitigating circumstance that should be taken into consideration? Though this last criterion may be difficult to judge, it is important to keep an open mind and a level of understanding with regard to employees' lives outside of work that may be affecting their attendance (e.g., an employee is dealing with major health issues or taking care of a sick family member).

Poor Performance

One of the most difficult aspects of a manager's job is dealing with poor employee performance. If managers are not trained properly or do not understand the organization's objectives, it will be difficult for them to determine an employee's performance level. The successful management of employee performance requires managers who are up-to-date with all immediate and long-term company objectives and who are continually observing their employees' performance. If work performance issues are not properly identified, brought to the attention of managers and employees, and then resolved, there may be increased costs for lost productivity, an increase in customer complaints, and lost profits. Sooner or later, to prevent any negative outcomes for the organization, every manager must deal with employees who perform poorly and do not respond to coaching or feedback. Sometimes poor performance is so serious that it requires immediate intervention.

Insubordination

The willingness of employees to carry out managers' directives is essential to a business's effective operation. When an employee refuses to obey a direct order from a supervisor, he or she is challenging the management's right to run the company. Insubordination also occurs when an employee is verbally abusive to a supervisor. Knowing how to handle these situations when they arise can help to avoid legal issues when an employee must be disciplined or even terminated. The last thing any organization wants is to have an upset employee refusing to do what he or she is supposed to, then later filing suit against the company because management did not handle the situation properly. A good start in dealing with insubordination is to talk with the employee in private, find out why he or she refuses to do a task, and then work together to find a resolution.

Alcohol-Related Misconduct

Two separate challenges are presented to managers by employees' use of alcohol. First, there is the challenge of managing an employee who is an alcoholic. Second, there is the challenge of managing an employee who uses alcohol or is intoxicated on the job.

The first step in dealing with either situation is to offer the employee help. The problem with this offer, however, is that many of these employees will deny that they have a problem and refuse assistance or treatment. From a business standpoint, it is important to document any instances or situations in which alcohol has played a role in the employee's lack of performance or his or her insubordinate actions. Keeping such records is necessary in making a case for disciplinary action, although this does not mean that you should give up on the employee: continue to offer help and treatment. Many people who have this problem experience denial, so it is difficult to get them to understand the severity of the situation, both with regard to their own personal health and with regard to their employment status. The disease can be so strong at times that the person is not able to see what is really happening or how serious his or her issues with alcohol may have become.

That being said, organizations still need to continue to do what is in the best interests of the company and take the appropriate course of action in holding the employee accountable for his or her performance or conduct. Therefore, at some point, it may be necessary to terminate the individual's employment.

Illegal Drug Use and Abuse

The problems associated with drug use are very similar to those associated with the use of alcohol. The primary difference is that the use of illegal drugs is prohibited by law, whereas the use of alcohol in moderation is socially acceptable. All employees within organizations deserve to work in an environment that is free from the effects of drug users and the problems they may bring.

In accordance with federal and state laws, and because of the potential detriment to the health and well-being of employees, all employees (including full-time, part-time, temporary, and intermittent) are prohibited from engaging in the unlawful use, possession, manufacture, distribution, dispensation, and sale of controlled substances.

Preventing the Need for Discipline with Human Resource Management

By properly designing human resource management systems, managers can eliminate a substantial amount of employee activity that would require disciplinary action and, in turn, limit the amount of time and effort spent on problems associated with implementing discipline. This can be done by communicating the company's established rules and procedures to all employees from the time they are hired, so that they understand what is expected of them from the start with regard to their performance and conduct.

Recruitment and Selection

As discussed earlier in the book, recruitment is a tool and a process by which organizations can identify and attract potential job candidates from either outside or inside the company and evaluate them for employment. Once all candidates have been identified, the process of selecting the appropriate candidates for employment can begin. This process starts with the collection, measurement, and evaluation of information about these candidates and their qualifications for specified positions. This is a great tool used by organizations to help them ensure that they are choosing the most qualified candidates with the right skills, abilities, and attitude to allow them to perform successfully in their target job. By spending more time and resources on recruiting and selection, managers can make better staffing decisions, hopefully avoiding those employees that may prove to be disciplinary problems once they enter their position.

Training and Development

Within human resource management, training and development are the activities that organizations use to help improve the performance of individuals and groups within the company, building on employees' strengths and introducing new ones.

Training focuses on improving an employee's performance in a specific job, while education focuses on providing an employee with the skills or knowledge that he or she may need for a position in the future. Both training and education are forms of employee development that are designed to help employees perform their current tasks while preparing for future positions.

By investing in training and development today, managers can reduce the likelihood of having large numbers of incompetent or obsolete employees in the future. In this way, organizations can combat poor performance, or the potential for it, before it starts.

 PROBLEM 11-3

What role should HR specialists play in ensuring that employees follow a company's code of ethics? How should ethics violations be disciplined?

 SOLUTION

The HR department should establish policies, rules, and procedures that are supportive of the ethics code. It should also create a climate that allows employees to report ethics violations without jeopardizing their job status. It should ensure that all complaints are effectively and efficiently investigated, by law if necessary, and handled properly moving forward.

Human Resource Planning

Just as human resource planning and strategy are vital if an organization is to achieve its overall strategic objectives, they are also necessary as precautionary measures in managing difficult employees, implementing disciplinary actions, and hopefully preventing behavior that creates such situations in the first place. Human resource planning illustrates throughout the organization that employees understand and are on board with the organization's policies and desired direction for the future. Strategically designed plans to support other functional areas of the organization, such as the marketing, finance, operation, and research and development departments, go a long way in helping to capture the people element of an organization, and can be utilized to avoid disruptive or insubordinate behavior that may be a result of employees' dissatisfaction with the company.

In the long term, human resource planning aims to match the right people with the right jobs and ensure that the organization has the appropriate mix of skills in its employees. By helping employees to develop their knowledge and skills, human resources seeks to create a better, more productive work environment. Overall, planning as such will hopefully alleviate disciplinary problems or difficult employee behavior before it becomes an issue. If human resource planning is successful in hiring and developing the right people, employees throughout the organization will demonstrate the appropriate attitudes and behaviors necessary to support the company's objectives. Furthermore, if utilized properly, HR planning can ensure that employees' job experiences are motivating, challenging, and satisfying, resulting in a reduction in poor performance problems that managers need to confront.

Performance Appraisal

Performance appraisal is the process of obtaining, analyzing, and recording information about the relative worth of an employee to the organization. Managers and supervisors need to analyze employees' successes and failures, along with their strengths and weaknesses, to determine whether further training is required or whether they may be eligible for promotion. By creating effective performance appraisal systems, managers can communicate their expectations and necessary performance improvements. In their employee development efforts, organizations' performance appraisals help guide and manage employees' behaviors.

A common approach to assessing the performance of employees is to rate them numerically against a list of objectives and attributes. In some companies, employees receive assessments from their manager, peers, subordinates, and customers, while also performing a self-assessment. This is known as a 360-degree appraisal and helps form good communication patterns, creating a more productive work environment that is less prone to disciplinary or poor performance issues.

Chapter Summary

Proper management hinges on the ability to provide corrective action should an employee not meet expectations. It should be noted that "discipline" is best provided in its most developmental form in order to allow the employee the opportunity to improve his or her performance. Properly managing the discipline process not only allows firms to improve their employees' performance, but also provides a documented "paper trail" to help protect them from potential unfair dismissal claims. Human resource management can effectively combat the issue of poor performance and the need for disciplinary actions by taking the initial steps in the recruitment, selection, and development of employees. Human resource planning and effective performance appraisal systems are major tools in maintaining a productive and satisfied workforce, one in which disciplinary problems will be faced less frequently.

QUIZ

1. Which of the following *is not* one of the three basic standards of discipline?
   A. Communication of criteria
   B. Documentation of facts
   C. Responding according to the employee's history
   D. Consistent response to infractions

2. Which of the following *is not* one of the three basic standards of discipline
   A. Swift justice
   B. Communication of criteria
   C. Documentation of facts
   D. Consistent response to infractions

3. When dealing with a poorly performing employee, a manager should
   A. Immediately fire the employee.
   B. Refer the problem to HR.
   C. Ignore the poor performance and give the employee another opportunity to succeed.
   D. Begin a progressive discipline process with the employee.

4. Encouraging employees to monitor their own behavior and assume responsibility for their actions is called
   A. Self-management.
   B. Positive discipline.
   C. Professional ethics.
   D. A bad idea.

5. Which of the following *is not* one of the possible steps in a progressive discipline program?
   A. Verbal warning
   B. Termination
   C. Probationary appeal
   D. Written warning

6. The just cause standard of discipline
   A. Allows for at-will dismissal.
   B. Protects employees from unfair termination.
   C. Places the burden of proof on the employee.
   D. Replaces company policies and rules.

7. **Positive discipline**
   A. Is not as effective as punitive discipline.
   B. Removes the fear of punishment.
   C. Helps build trust within an organization.
   D. Deemphasizes the influence of management.

8. **When an employee refuses to obey a direct order from a supervisor, it is a direct challenge of management's right to run the company. This is considered to be**
   A. Misconduct.
   B. Poor performance.
   C. Insubordination.
   D. Delinquency.

9. **The process of analyzing information about the relative worth of an employee's contributions to the organization is called**
   A. Performance appraisal.
   B. Career development.
   C. Training opportunities.
   D. Productivity review.

10. **Which of the following *is not* a step that might be used in disciplining a difficult employee?**
    A. Ignoring the undesirable behavior
    B. Examining the facts of the situation
    C. Confronting the employee to discuss the situation
    D. Looking at the situation from both sides

chapter **12**

Employee Separation, Downsizing, and Outplacement

This chapter covers the concepts of outplacement, downsizing, and employee separation. In today's business world, more than ever before, there is an ever-present fear of downsizing, termination, or loss of high-performing talent. These situations, in combination with many others, make up the set of forms of employee separation. An employee separation occurs when an employee ceases to be a member of an organization. The rate of employee separations in an organization, also known as the turnover rate, is a measure of the rate at which employees leave the firm.

CHAPTER OBJECTIVES

After completing this chapter, the student should be able to

1. Understand the cost of employee separation.

2. Understand the difference between voluntary and involuntary turnover.

3. Understand and determine how to define layoff criteria.

4. Understand layoff alternatives and outplacement.

Employee Turnover

As you traverse corporate America, the "turnover rate" is discussed ad nauseam as something to be "managed" or "contained"; however, sometimes loss of talent, dismissal, or employee layoffs are inevitable. There are many costs, benefits, and ethical considerations for the HR manager when dealing with employee separation.

There are a number of costs associated with employee separations, which may be greater or smaller depending on whether managers intend to eliminate the position or to replace the departing employee. Separation costs include

- Separated employee costs
- Recruitment costs
- Selection costs
- Training costs

While this may perhaps be intuitive, when making the decision to dismiss, lay off, or terminate an employee, these costs can be prohibitive. Also to be considered is the cost of lost productivity while the position is vacant, as well as lost productivity for those employees who are participating in the replacement hiring process, taking time and effort away from their normal job activities.

While many people understand the costs of employee separations, there can be benefits as well. Some of the benefits of separations include

- Reduced labor costs
- Replacement of poor performers
- Increased innovation
- Opportunity for greater diversity

When an individual leaves an organization, whether on good or bad terms, it is important to frame the situation in a positive way, emphasizing that it is an opportunity for the organization. As noted earlier, increased productivity and innovation, along with the infusion of new ideas, can bring new life to an organizational unit that is mired in low performance and low morale. While losing high-performing employees or well-liked coworkers can be daunting, it also provides an opportunity for other employees to "step up to the plate" and reach new levels of their potential. In addition, infusing new blood into the organization with an external hire can benefit the existing employees and managers, and the company as a whole.

Types of Employee Separations

Employee separations can be divided into two categories based on who initiates the termination of the employment relationship. Voluntary separations (quits and retirements) are initiated by the employee. Involuntary separations (discharges and layoffs) are initiated by the employer.

Voluntary Separations

An Employee Leaves an Organization of His or Her Own Accord

Voluntary separations of this type can be minimized through equitable compensation, benefits programs, and the creation of strong links between the employee and the organization. While some quits can be avoided, the circumstances surrounding many employee quits are completely beyond the control of the organization (e.g., the relocation of a spouse or a change in family dynamics or size).

An Employee Retires

Retirement can be a double-edged sword for an organization and its productivity. Some retiring senior workers have high salaries and may be replaceable by less expensive and often more productive junior employees. In such situations, organizations are likely to offer "early retirement" incentives to older employees whose maximum productivity level may not be as great as others'. However, the organizational knowledge held by senior employees is difficult to harness, and it may take junior employees years to achieve the understanding of the organization and its systems that the senior employees possess. In addition, loyalty and dedication for a long period of time is something that should be celebrated, not only to show gratitude for the employee who has stayed with the organization for many years, but also to show more junior employees that the organization values longevity and commitment.

Involuntary Separations

Involuntary separations occur when management decides to terminate its relationship with an employee because of either economic necessity or a poor fit between the employee and the organization. Examples of involuntary separations include discharges, layoffs, and downsizing or "right"-sizing (a term used by firms to make downsizing appear more palatable, generally positioning it as an attempt to make the firm the "right" size for its needs by implementing layoffs).

PROBLEM 12-1

What can a company do to help a community when it decides to close a plant that is important to the community's economic prosperity?

SOLUTION

There are several things that a company can do to assist a community that will be affected by its decision to close a plant. One major item is early notification. In fact, before the final decision is made, the possibility has usually been discussed for several years. Some companies have begun to signal communities that they are considering such actions several years before actually making a move. This gives the community time to try to attract alternative employers and to prepare for the economic impact of the company's departure.

Also, in some cases, members of the community may seek a buyer for the plant. If such overtures are made, it is in the best interests of both the company and the community to reach an agreement in a timely and reasonable fashion. Alternatively, the community may seek ways to help the company regain the profitability it needs from the plant if it is to keep it in operation. Sometimes the company may need increased employee productivity, and other times it may need to receive some type of tax relief or other benefits that can be granted by the community. In general, the best thing a company can do is communicate clearly and early, then work with the community to develop innovative alternatives.

Layoffs

Generally, an organization will institute a layoff when it cannot reduce its labor costs by any other means. Managers should first try to reduce their labor costs with alternatives to layoffs. It is also important to note that layoffs have a large emotional component. As many individuals derive their identity and their sense of self-worth from their jobs, the sudden loss or instability of their jobs can result in serious distress, and also in dissatisfaction and a decrease in productivity if for those employees who are still at the company. For this reason, the responsible manager has a duty to explore all alternatives to layoffs before implementing them.

There are many alternative methods of reducing labor costs that management should explore before deciding to conduct a layoff. These alternatives include the following:

- *Changes in job design.* It is entirely possible that redesigning jobs might allow for a reduction in the number of necessary layoffs by decreasing unit cost and/or increasing output.

- *Pay and benefits policies.* On occasion, alterations in employer benefits contributions, job sharing, or shifting from a full-time to a part-time workforce can alleviate financial stress. While such moves are not ideal, employees will at least have some level of income compared to zero income from a full layoff.

- *Training.* Employees can sometimes be cross-trained to perform multiple jobs, thereby reducing costs, or, alternatively, training in general can be put on hold in order to reduce costs.

There are additional alternatives to layoffs, including early retirements and nontraditional options.

Early Retirements

When a company realizes that it needs to downsize its scale of operations, its first task is to examine alternatives to layoffs. One of the most popular of these methods is early retirement.

Early retirement policies consist of two features: (1) a package of financial incentives that make it attractive for senior employees to retire earlier than they had planned, and (2) an open window that restricts eligibility for these incentives to a fairly short period. After the window is closed, the incentives are no longer available to senior employees.

Managing early retirement policies requires careful design, implementation, and administration. All managers dealing with senior employees should make certain that they do not treat them any differently from other employees when approaching them about the potential situation. When not properly managed, early retirement policies can create a host of problems.

Nontraditional Alternatives to Layoffs

Job sharing, voluntary or involuntary furloughs, across-the-board pay reductions, and use of unpaid leave are just a few of the alternatives that might be considered in place of laying off employees. It is important to note that employees themselves are often the best source of creative alternatives to layoffs. Open and honest exchanges about financial reality not only empower employees but give them an opportunity to provide direction for the company and feel more satisfied at work.

PROBLEM 1 2-2

How much notice of a layoff should a company be obligated to give?

SOLUTION

While federal law now requires U.S. employers with more than 100 employees to give 60 days' advance notice of layoffs that will affect an entire plant or 50 or more employees, there are many layoffs that do not meet this criterion. Focus on those layoffs that are not covered by this regulation.

Some may argue that employers should give as much notice as possible, letting employees know as soon as it becomes clear that this step will need to be taken. However, layoffs have many other impacts, including their effects on stock prices, competitor advantages, and general organization issues, that may make an employer unwilling to provide early advance notice. Others may argue that advance notice is much less important than a good severance package that will allow the employee time to search for another job.

Implementing a Layoff

Implementing a layoff is something that is easier said than done. Many times the economic viability of a layoff makes sense, but the interpersonal component of actually laying off an employee can be incredibly difficult. In the unfortunate event that a layoff must occur, the individual performing the layoff must be prepared for the fallout and emotional response associated with a change in job status. A layoff can be a traumatic event that affects the lives of thousands of people, so managers must implement the layoff carefully. Issues that need to be considered include the following:

- *Notifying employees.* Develop a plan by asking how employees will be notified. Consider what options for returning they will be given and what information should, and should not, be shared. It is especially important to consider how the employees might react to the difficult news.

- *Developing layoff criteria.* Clear criteria, sometimes dictated by union contracts when working with organized labor, should be communicated and applied fairly across all employees.

- *Communicating with laid-off employees.* Sharing of information in the layoff process should be as open and honest as possible. A lack of information can lead to problems with "survivors" of the layoff and, should employees return after a period of layoff, may have created a sense of distrust of management. If employees understand the circumstances and the layoff criteria, they are less likely to react to the decision in a destructive manner.

- *Coordinating media relations.* As stated earlier in the text, HR is sometimes PR (public relations). When a firm can "control the message" and provide the media with factual information in a timely and even-handed form, the press is less likely to jump to conclusions about the layoff or create negative news stories.

- *Maintaining security.* It is important to provide for the well-being of the survivors of the layoff, both physically and emotionally, and let them know that their positions are secure. In addition, as some employees may have extreme reactions to news of a layoff, providing security for the safety of all is prudent.

Still Struggling

Layoffs, outplacement, and early retirement should all be alternatives that the successful organization does not need to implement. However, it is important to be aware of the options available to decrease the costs associated with employees. Many times efficiencies in labor costs are governed by union or other employment contracts. Be certain to consider these contractual rights should it be necessary to eliminate workers or combine existing positions.

Outplacement

Outplacement is a human resource program that is created to help separated employees deal with the emotional stress of job loss and to provide them with assistance in finding a new position. In some cases, when a firm is restructuring or downsizing, the recruiting function will be turned "inside out" to help displaced employees find other employment. When this is possible, not only is it the "right" thing to do, but it also creates goodwill in the community at large and can make corporate restructuring more palatable to the general public.

The goals of outplacement reflect the organization's need to maintain employee productivity from both survivors and those who will be displaced. The most important of these goals are: (1) reducing the morale problems of employees who will be laid off so that they will remain productive until the layoff occurs, (2) minimizing the amount of litigation initiated by separated employees, and (3) assisting separated employees in quickly finding comparable jobs.

The most common outplacement services provided to separated employees are emotional support and job-search assistance and can range from employee assistance plan—like on-site counseling to direct recruiting efforts like those mentioned earlier.

In sum, while restructuring, downsizing or right-sizing, and outplacement can be painful, they are a reality in the turbulent world of corporate America. As dramatic changes can influence the psychological well-being of individual employees and affect the economic prosperity of the communities involved, it is important to explore all alternatives and properly manage downsizing efforts when they are deemed necessary.

 PROBLEM 12-3

Is it ethical for top managers to receive cash bonuses while at the same time asking lower-level employees to accept a pay freeze?

 SOLUTION

Most people will respond that this is not acceptable or ethical behavior on the part of top managers. At the most basic level, it will certainly not create a sense of loyalty among the employees, who will find the practice unfair.

Chapter Summary

Layoffs, outplacement, downsizing, right-sizing, and the like are all terms that an HR manager never wants to hear. Though they are some of the most difficult and unpleasant programs to implement in the corporate world, they are nonetheless becoming more and more common in today's convulsive economic landscape. Being prepared, communicating effectively, and making the maximum effort to provide for your employees are common-sense, yet all too often overlooked strategies that HR managers must use if they are to weather the storm should the day arrive when layoffs or downsizing becomes necessary. While rarely appreciated, HR can play a significant role in limiting the hardship and discomfort associated with the implementation of a reduction in force or a temporary change in employment status.

QUIZ

1. **All but which of the following are costs associated with employee separations?**
   A. Recruitment costs
   B. Selection costs
   C. Development costs
   D. Separated employee costs

2. **Which of the following is considered a voluntary separation?**
   A. Layoff
   B. Resignation
   C. Downsizing
   D. Discharge for cause

3. **Generally, an organization will institute a layoff when**
   A. It cannot reduce its costs by any other means.
   B. The organization has identified low-performing employees.
   C. An employee continually receives poor performance evaluations.
   D. An employee fails an alcohol or drug screening.

4. **Which of the following are alternatives to layoffs?**
   A. Employment policies
   B. Changes in job design
   C. Pay and benefits policies
   D. All of the above

5. **A human resource program that is created to help separated employees deal with the emotional stress of job loss and to provide assistance in finding a new job is**
   A. Layoff counseling.
   B. An employee assistance program.
   C. Outplacement.
   D. Unemployment.

6. **Which of the following is *not* a benefit of employee separations?**
   A. Increased labor costs
   B. Replacement of poor performers
   C. Increased innovation
   D. Opportunity for greater diversity

7. Which of these is *not* true about early retirement?
    A. It is not a good alternative to layoffs.
    B. It includes a package of financial incentives to attract senior employees.
    C. The open window of eligibility is short.
    D. It can cause a host of problems if it is not properly managed.

8. Which of the following is an appropriate response to a laid-off employee?
    A. "It's not the end of the world."
    B. "Consider this a blessing in disguise."
    C. "It's just a job."
    D. "I can see you are upset. Is there someone I can call for you?"

9. When you are preparing to inform an employee of a layoff, it is best to
    A. Choose a public place where others are around in case the employee becomes angry.
    B. If possible, inform the employee immediately prior to a scheduled vacation.
    C. Consider the day in relationship to a significant day for the employee, i.e., a birthday, anniversary, or something similar.
    D. Plan to be concise and keep the conversation brief.

10. Outplacement firms can assist laid-off employees by
    A. Holding mock interviews.
    B. Critiquing résumés.
    C. Both a and b.
    D. None of the above.

chapter **13**

Working with Organized Labor

Dealing with organized labor strikes fear into the heart of many an HR professional, but it need not be a scary undertaking. It should be noted that parts of this chapter apply only to firms in "union" states and not necessarily to those in "right to work" states. Union states are those in which union membership is mandatory for certain jobs. There are also 22 "right-to-work" states in the United States where, in accordance with the Taft-Hartley Act, workers are not required to join a union as a condition of employment. Please check the specific union laws of the state(s) in which your firm operates before making any decisions or policies that will affect organized labor. This chapter will discuss the labor-organizing process and present an overview of the legislation governing actions such as the collective bargaining process and grievances.

CHAPTER OBJECTIVES

After completing this chapter, the student should be able to

1. Understand the basic tenets of the Wagner Act, the Taft-Hartley Act, and the Landrum-Griffin Act.

2. Describe the collective bargaining process.

3. Understand how labor might organize and how management should respond.

The Origins of U.S. Labor Unions

A union is an organization that represents employees' interests in negotiating with management on issues such as wages, hours, and working conditions. Unions are a separate entity from the organization's management, and the services they provide to their members are paid for by union dues. The most basic reason that employees join unions is to help them guarantee that they have a safe, secure work environment. More specifically, employees will seek to join a union when they (1) are dissatisfied with certain aspects of their job, (2) feel a lack of power or influence with management in terms of making changes, and (3) see unionization as a solution to their problems at work.

Unions, as we know them today, were largely unprotected by law in the United States until the passing of the Wagner Act in 1935, which gave workers the right to organize. During the Great Depression (1930s), millions of workers lost their jobs as employers cut production costs. Consequently, unions were widely supported because workers were regarded as having little power.

In recent years, however, the public perception of unions has changed dramatically. Unions have come to be regarded by many people as having too much power; therefore, when unionized workers face challenges, there is little sympathy from the public. While unions do a great deal of positive work, many negative issues, such as corruption and abuse of power by union leaders, have been widely covered in the media.

Managers are on the front lines in dealing with employee or labor-management matters, so it is imperative that organizations carefully train members of management who deal with such employees. Unions have a responsibility to their members to inform management of any issues and concerns that their organized workers may be facing. In addition, management must consult with unions before giving any sort of pay increases to unionized employees, largely because of the seniority system that unions follow, in which organizational tenure, not performance, dictates pay increases. This situation takes a great deal of control away from a company. Management may also face constraints when disciplining a union employee. Because of these challenges, when a union enters the picture, labor relations specialists are hired to resolve grievances, negotiate a labor contract, and advise top management on labor relations strategy.

Labor relations policy is based on three laws: the Wagner Act (National Labor Relations Act of 1935), the Taft-Hartley Act (Labor Management Relations

Act of 1947) and the Landrum-Griffin Act (Labor-Management Reporting and Disclosure Act of 1959).

 PROBLEM 13-1

What factors are encouraging unions and management in the United States to adopt more cooperative strategies today?

 SOLUTION

The factors that are encouraging unions and management to adopt more cooperative strategies today include (1) the trend toward employee involvement, (2) both sharing the same general interest (a profitable enterprise) and experiencing greater security and rewards through cooperation, (3) external developments, such as automation and global competition, that require a competitive advantage, which can be produced through cooperation, (4) an increasingly educated workforce, (5) the highly publicized legal problems of some union leaders, and (6) shrinking union membership.

The Wagner Act

The National Labor Relations Act (NLRA), or the Wagner Act, was passed in 1935. It established the National Labor Relations Board (NLRB) and prohibited five labor practices:

1. Interfering with employees' right to form unions
2. Interfering with the administration of a union
3. Discriminating against union members
4. Discriminating against an employee who has filed charges under the act
5. Refusing to bargain with the union

The NLRB's primary functions today are to administer certification elections and prevent unfair labor practices. A certification election is a practice in which the employees' support for unionization is demonstrated based on the number of employees within a company that vote in favor of organizing. Should unfair labor practices occur, the NLRB issues a cease and desist order to stop such practices. The NLRB is also responsible for determining whether a proposed bargaining unit is appropriate (discussed later in this chapter in the section, "Collective Bargaining").

The Taft-Hartley Act

Also known as the Labor Management Relations Act (LMRA), the Taft-Hartley Act was passed in 1947 to limit some of the powers that unions had acquired under the Wagner Act. One of the major attributes of the act for employers is that it allows them to file charges of unfair labor practices against unions. The Taft-Hartley Act outlines six unfair labor practices by unions:

1. Coercing employees
2. Causing the employer to discriminate against nonunion members
3. Refusing to bargain in good faith
4. Secondary boycotts
5. Excessive dues
6. Featherbedding (when unions cause employers to pay for services that were not performed)

In addition to these unfair labor practices, there are a number of other major provisions of the Taft-Hartley Act, including the following:

- *Right-to-work law.* This is a state law that makes it illegal within a particular state for a union shop clause, which requires all workers to be (or become) union members, to be included in a union contract.
- *Union shops.* In a union-shop situation, a new employee is required to become a member of the union as a condition of being hired. Taft-Hartley protects employees in right-to-work states from having to join; the act is not able to do so in union states.
- *Decertification election.* This provision allows unionized employees to eliminate the union to which they belong.
- *Creation of the Federal Mediation and Conciliation Service.* This service mediates labor disputes so that the economic burden of strikes and labor disturbances is minimized.

The Landrum-Griffin Act

This act, also called the Labor-Management Reporting and Disclosure Act (LMRDA), was passed in 1959 to give union members rights against and protections from their union leadership. It also protects the rights of union members against corrupt or discriminatory labor unions. The act established five key provisions:

1. There is a bill of rights for union members.
2. A union must have a constitution.
3. A union must report its financial activities.
4. Union elections are regulated by the government.
5. Fiduciary responsibility is required of union leaders.

In addition to these three main acts, the Railway Labor Act of 1926 is also important because, at the time, it gave railroad workers the right to organize and bargain collectively. Today, the name of the act is misleading, as it not only continues to cover rail workers, but now also covers other transportation workers, including airline employees.

Labor Relations

Labor relations in the United States evolved from within the capitalist economic structure. The key factors that characterize labor relations in this country today are business unionism, unions structured by type of job, collective bargaining, labor contracts, adversarial labor-management relations, and increased unionism in the public sector.

Unions in the United States put a high priority on improving the economic welfare of their members. Business unionism focuses on "bread-and-butter" issues such as wages, benefits, and job security. U.S. labor laws reinforce these key issues, and management is obligated to deal with unions in good faith.

Unlike unions in some other countries, U.S. unions tend to be organized by type of job. For example, autoworkers, teachers, electricians, and plumbers each have their own union. A major union for electricians is the International Brotherhood of Electrical Workers (IBEW). IBEW has members from the United States, Canada, and the Pacific Islands. In addition to national unions, there are small local unions that deal with members in their specific geographic locations.

Collective Bargaining

Collective bargaining can be defined as the process by which union and management reach an agreement regarding the work rules (pay, grievances, leave, and so on) and terms of the employees' work. In the collective bargaining process, "units" make labor agreements with their employers. The NLRB determines whether or not the breadth of these units is appropriate. For example, autoworkers are part of one unit, and firefighters or police might be part of another unit. However, a unit never consists of a group of employees from disparate positions across an organization. They are, instead, generally organized by occupation.

The product of collective bargaining is a labor contract that spells out the conditions of employment and work rules that affect employees in the unit represented by the union. If one of the involved parties does not fulfill its responsibilities as detailed in the contract, legal action can be taken. U.S. labor laws view labor and management as natural adversaries who will disagree over the distribution of the firm's profits. For this reason, rules have been put in place so that the "pie," or profits, is distributed peacefully.

Current Union Membership

Union membership as a whole has continued to decline in recent years. This situation is commonly attributed to the younger generation of workers being increasingly educated and less "trade" focused. Also, because of the increased protection of employees under federal and state employment laws, many workers do not feel the necessity to join a union.

Following the overall declining trend, the percentage of workers in the private sector who are unionized has fallen; however, in the public sector, the percentage unionized has actually increased substantially. Nonetheless, even with this increase in public-sector union participation, the unionized employees have less power than union members in the past because of the government's recent strength and influence. Many governmental employees are also forbidden to strike.

Labor Relations around the Globe

Labor relations systems differ from country to country, with "unionization" having different meanings, and implying different roles, in various places. Trends in the United States are not the same as those throughout the world. For example, while private-sector unions are decreasing in the United States, they still make up a large portion of the unions worldwide.

Some unions emphasize economic issues, while others focus on political issues. Also, some unions will emphasize both, while other unions will not consider either of these areas to be a main concern. U.S. unions tend to focus heavily on economic issues, whereas unions in countries like Spain and France emphasize political issues heavily. Because of China's being under the control of a Communist government, neither economic issues nor political ones are emphasized. Swedish trade unions, however, are involved in both areas. Highlighted in the following sections are two unique union situations: Germany's and Japan's.

Germany

Germany's industrial democracy uses works councils and codetermination. Works councils are groups in which representatives of both management and workers join together to make decisions on important issues such as operational procedures, employee discipline, and training. They also work to ensure responsible governing of the workplace. Codetermination has created cooperation between workers and management by assembling worker representatives to bring issues to the attention of the corporate board leadership.

Japan

Japan's enterprise union has been a key factor in the success of the country's labor relations. The union is made up of workers from different industries, and also some members of management. Union members tend to stay in the union for the entire duration of their careers, as the union covers multiple industries and companies. There is a high level of cooperation and respect between organizations and the enterprise union, which only adds to its successes.

Labor Relations Strategy

The most important strategic choice affecting a company's labor relations is management's strategic decision to accept or to avoid unions.

Union Acceptance Strategy

This strategy accepts collective bargaining as an appropriate way of establishing work rules through an exclusive agent representing the employees. A company employing this strategy does not challenge the union's right to represent the employees. One major success factor in this situation is that committees are assembled to deal with long-term issues, creating what will hopefully be a positive and long-lasting relationship between the union and the company.

These committees have representation from both management and the union and contribute to a high level of cooperation.

Union Avoidance Strategy

An avoidance strategy is employed by those companies or groups that believe that unions have a disruptive influence on employees. Companies may choose from two approaches to implement this strategy:

1. *Union substitution.* With this approach, management addresses and resolves employee issues with a focus on satisfying employee needs.
2. *Union suppression.* In such a situation, management addresses employee complaints with severe action, such as replacing striking employees with nonunion employees or nearly threatening employees' job security if they attempt to unionize.

Although the aim of both strategies is to keep workers from organizing, the substitution strategy attempts to placate employees and provide assistance, while the suppression strategy employs a much more hard-line approach. Today, most companies that are attempting to avoid what they consider union disturbances employ the substitution strategy.

Managing Labor Relations

There are three phases to the labor relations process: (1) union organizing, (2) collective bargaining (negotiating), and (3) contract administration. As each of these areas is quite difficult to manage, labor relations specialists are often employed to manage, maintain, and oversee these processes.

Union Organizing

The union organizing phase is the first step, in which employees work with a union to form themselves into a cohesive group. In union solicitation, a minimum of 30 percent of the company's employees must sign an authorization card indicating which union they would like to have represent them.

Next, a certification election must take place, in which employees determine whether or not they will organize. As mentioned, the NLRB generally conducts the election. For unionization to move forward, a majority of employees must indicate their preference for unionizing via polling at their place of work. The NLRB, the union, and the company's management all are allowed reasonable observation of the polling. Various processes are also in place to challenge the results of the election should any party desire to do so.

Management cannot threaten employees who are considering unionization. Nor can employers promise benefits that imitate union objectives (e.g., managers claiming that unionization is worthless, since the company will "take care of them" with regard to benefits, work conditions, and other such factors if they do not join) in an attempt to steer employees clear of union participation. Furthermore, management cannot spy on unionization meetings.

Collective Bargaining

As discussed earlier in the chapter, a collective bargaining system is one in which the union and management negotiate with each other to develop the work rules. It is assumed that all parties will deal in good faith when discussing all topics, such as wages, hours, and employment conditions. The result of the discussion will be in favor of the party who holds the most bargaining power and has the ability to get the other party to agree to its terms, although concessions may be made by both sides in order to come to a conclusion that will please everyone. Impasses in the bargaining process will occur if an agreement between the two parties cannot be reached.

Contract Administration

The key aspect of contract administration is the management of the contract and the grievance procedure. The most typical types of grievances involve contract interpretation issues and employee discipline situations.

The first step in the grievance procedure involves the employee relaying his or her grievance to the union steward (most issues are typically resolved with this first step). If the issue is not resolved at that time, the grievance is put in writing, and the parties have five working days to resolve the issue. After a process of negotiations involving the employee, management, and the union, arbitration takes place in hopes that a reasonable agreement satisfying all parties will be reached.

A grievance procedure not only helps to resolve issues in an efficient manner, but also ensures that justice is served. The procedure causes upper management to consider the issues that arise, not only with regard to the current, specific problem, but also with regard to how to deal with such a problem before it occurs again in the future.

HRM and Union Employees

Managers would prefer to develop HRM policies based on efficiency, but when a union is involved, these policies must reflect the employees' preferences as well. Employees have preferences related to staffing, employee development, compensation, and employee relations.

The contract between managers and unions can dictate how jobs are filled and on what basis they are filled. Layoffs, merit, and seniority are factors that must be considered when making staffing decisions.

Performance evaluations are rarely used in unionized organizations. However, there is often a greater amount of worker training. Because a large majority of the unions are based on trades, the unions invest time and money in worker training, which, in turn, helps the organization retain those workers. Some unions now offer educational courses for employees who did not complete their basic education.

On average, union employees earn 10 to 20 percent higher wages than comparable nonunion employees. Unionized firms avoid using merit pay plans and are likely to give employees across-the-board pay raises based on market considerations. A cost-of-living adjustment, where employees receive additional pay to counterbalance inflation, is a common type of pay raise. Unions also frequently offer valuable benefit packages to their members and contribute to ensuring that legally required benefits are enforced.

The labor contract gives employees specific rights. The employees, through the collective bargaining process, have a voice in the development of work rules that affect their jobs. Issues that may arise are typically resolved using the grievance procedures, which help to avoid court time and costs. If issues are not resolved using this method and an investigation ensues, union employees have the right to have a coworker present when dealing with an investigation that could lead to disciplinary action. This right is known as a *Weingarten right*, which was established by the NLRA.

 PROBLEM 13-2

What factors explain why unions in the United States have been losing more than 50 percent of all certification elections?

 SOLUTION

There are several reasons why unions have been losing so many certification elections. First, management styles have changed in the past 15 to 20

years as the workforce has become more transient. This situation has created more employee involvement, empowerment, and other elements that make employees feel that they do not need collective bargaining. Second, there has been a decline in industrial jobs and an increase in service industry jobs. Many service industry employees do not tend to support unionization, but instead view it as something that is solely for industrial-type jobs. Third, unions have not been as successful at securing good contracts for their membership in the past 15 to 20 years.

Chapter Summary

Many HR professionals are uncomfortable when they are faced with the possibility of dealing with organized labor. As discussed in this chapter, while there are specific considerations that must be taken into account when dealing with unions, a skilled HR professional acting in a professional and ethical manner should have little trouble adhering to the required specifications. Overall, both HR and the union should, at bottom, have the best interests of the employees at the top of their priority list; if this is the case, organized labor and management should have a relatively harmonious relationship.

QUIZ

1. Which of the following is *not* one of the most common reasons that employees choose to join unions?
    A. They feel a lack of power or influence with management in terms of making changes.
    B. They are dissatisfied with aspects of their job.
    C. They see unionization as a solution to their problems.
    D. They are hired into a position that requires union membership.

2. Employee relationship specialists are hired to do all but which of the following?
    A. Resolve grievances
    B. Negotiate a labor contract
    C. Provide mediation between management and unions
    D. Advise top management on labor relations strategy

3. Labor relations policy is largely based on all but which of the following acts?
    A. Railroad Act of 1926
    B. Wagner Act of 1935
    C. Taft-Hartley Act of 1947
    D. Landrum-Griffin Act of 1959

4. Which of the following is prohibited under the Wagner Act?
    A. Refusing to bargain in good faith
    B. Featherbedding
    C. Refusing to bargain with the union
    D. Coercing employees

5. Which of the following is not a provision of the Landrum-Griffin Act?
    A. There is a bill of rights for union members.
    B. A union must have a constitution.
    C. Unions do not need to report their financial activities to the government.
    D. Elections are regulated by the government.

6. Which of the following is not one of the key factors that characterize labor relations in the United States?
    A. Decreased unionism in the public sector
    B. Collective bargaining
    C. Business unionism
    D. Union structure by type of job

7. Which of the following is prohibited under the Taft-Hartley Act?
   A. Interfering with employees' rights to form unions
   B. Discriminating against an employee who has filed charges under the act
   C. Refusing to bargain with the union
   D. Coercing employees

8. This strategy accepts collective bargaining as an appropriate way of establishing work rules through an exclusive agent for the employees.
   A. Labor relations strategy
   B. Union acceptance strategy
   C. Union avoidance strategy
   D. Union partnership strategy

9. Which of the following is not one of the three phases of the labor relations process?
   A. Union organizing
   B. Collective bargaining
   C. Contract administration
   D. Negotiations

10. On average, union employees earn what percentage more than comparable nonunion employees?
    A. 5 to 10 percent
    B. 15 to 25 percent
    C. 10 to 20 percent
    D. 25 to 30 percent

Final Exam

1. Which of the following is not one of the four basic functions of management?

   A. Staffing **B.** Leading **C.** Organizing **D.** Developing

2. Which of the following statements about Title VII of the Civil Rights Act is true?

   A. All employees must have equal working conditions. **B.** Discrimination on the basis of race and sexual orientation is prohibited. **C.** Employers must provide sexual harassment training for all employees. **D.** Employees must have an equal opportunity to participate in training.

3. In human resource management, evolving work and family roles is considered this type of challenge.

   A. Individual **B.** Managerial **C.** Environmental **D.** Organizational

4. Which key factors should firms consider in determining which HR strategies will have a positive impact on a firm's performance?

   A. Organizational strategies, characteristics, capabilities, and the environment **B.** Organizational structure and systems **C.** Organizational resources and capabilities **D.** Organizational structure and competitor key success factors

5. HR strategies must align with

   A. Organizational strategic thinking. **B.** Organizational characteristics and capabilities. **C.** Both organizational strategies and the external environment. **D.** Organizational tactics and a strategic lens.

6. Corporate strategy can be defined as

    A. Strategy among the established firms or units of the corporation.
    B. Organizational exploitation of leadership strategy, differentiation, and competitive advantage. C. The mix of businesses that a corporation decides to hold and the flow of resources among those businesses.
    D. Organizational strategic tactics to gain market share among competitors.

7. According to the Age Discrimination in Employment Act, which of the following statements is true

    A. High-level managers have no mandatory requirements for retirement.
    B. A company may discontinue pension accruals for employees over age 65. C. Employers may fire an employee over age 40 for good cause.
    D. Employers do not need to offer insurance to employees who are covered by Medicare.

8. In HR management, clashing views about ethics and responsibility are considered this type of challenge:

    A. Individual B. Managerial C. Environmental D. Organizational

9. The Age Discrimination in Employment Act of 1967 protects individuals of or older than

    A. 30. B. 35. C. 40. D. 45.

10. Title VII of the Civil Rights Act of 1964 mandates that employment decisions may not be based on which of the following?

    A. Race, color, religion, sex, sexual orientation, or national origin B. Race, color, religion, ethnicity, sex, sexual orientation, or national origin C. Race, color, religion, sex, or national origin D. Race, color, ethnicity, sex, sexual orientation, or national origin

11. The Americans with Disabilities Act applies to

    A. Employers with more than 15 employees. B. Employers with more than 25 employees. C. Employers who contract with the federal government.
    D. All employers, regardless of the size of the company.

12. The Equal Pay Act of 1963 requires that

    A. Men and women are paid equally for similar work in all like organizations. B. Men and women receive the same pay if they do the same job in the same organization. C. Individuals receive similar pay for jobs within a similar grade of the organization. **D.** Individuals of a protected class are paid equally for similar work in all like organizations.

13. **Quid pro quo sexual harassment can best be defined in the following way:**

    A. The employee is required to engage in sexual activity in exchange for workplace entitlements or benefits. **B.** Harassment is unwelcome by the harassed person and becomes sufficiently severe or pervasive to create an abusive environment. **C.** An organization fails to require sexual harassment training for its employees and an incident occurs. **D.** Two parties willingly engage in sexual activity in the workplace.

14. **Which statement is true about quotas?**

    A. The percentage of women and/or minorities that an organization must hire to correct underrepresentation is based on availability in the geographic area. **B.** Employers must make a good faith effort to fulfill quotas set by their affirmative action plan. **C.** Employers are required to hire a person who helps them to reach a placement goal, whether or not there is a more qualified candidate. **D.** They are expressly forbidden.

15. **Adverse impact in action: Suppose 100 women and 100 men take a promotion examination, and 100 percent of the men and 50 percent of the women pass the exam. What percentage of the women would need to pass to comply with the four-fifths rule?**

    A. 50 percent **B.** 60 percent **C.** 70 percent **D.** 80 percent

16. **Under the Americans with Disabilities Act, which of the following statements is true?**

    A. Preemployment medical examinations may be required before a job offer is extended. **B.** Employers must set affirmative action plans for the disabled. **C.** Employers do not need to accommodate a disability if it results in undue hardship. **D.** Rehabilitated drug users are excluded by the law.

17. **Which minority group is often referred to as the "model minority"?**

    A. African Americans **B.** Asian Americans **C.** Hispanic Americans **D.** Arab Americans

18. **What form of discrimination is legally acceptable in the workplace?**

    A. Racial discrimination **B.** Sexual orientation discrimination **C.** Generational discrimination **D.** Gender discrimination

19. The Americans with Disabilities Act does not protect an employee who

    A. Uses illegal drugs. B. Has epilepsy. C. Has AIDS. D. Has serious psychological problems.

20. Discrimination against members of a dominant or majority group is referred to as

    A. Ableism. B. Egalitarianism. C. Reverse discrimination. D. Anglo-Saxon discrimination.

21. What piece of legislation was passed specifically to enforce the acceptance and equality of African Americans?

    A. Fair Labor Standards Act of 1938 B. Civil Rights Act of 1964 C. Jim Crow laws D. Equal Rights Amendment of 1972

22. Which of the following is not a type of contingent worker?

    A. College interns B. Temporary employees C. Full-time employees D. Contract workers

23. Which of the following procedurally assists employers in complying with federal regulations against discrimination?

    A. Executive Order 11246 B. Congressional Accountability Act C. Title VII of the Civil Rights Act D. Uniform Guidelines on Employee Selection Procedures

24. Which of the following is not one of the four key elements of a job description?

    A. Job summary B. Preferred qualifications C. Identification information D. Job specifications and minimum qualifications

25. Job characteristics theory can be defined as

    A. A theory that states that employee motivation depends on job characteristics such as skill variety, task identity, task significance, autonomy, and feedback. B. A theory that states that motivation and job satisfaction depend on the fit between the employee's abilities or needs and the job and organizational characteristics. C. A concept that talks about how to design a job so that it is simple for an employee. D. A concept that states that an employee will adapt to the job characteristics that he or she needs to, while eliminating unnecessary work.

26. Former General Electric chairman Jack Welch wanted to eliminate vertical and horizontal boundaries within the company and break down external barriers between the company and its customers and suppliers. What kind of organization design does this describe?

   A. Bureaucratic organization   B. Flat organization   C. Boundaryless organization   D. Centralized organization

27. Organizations are following the trend of outsourcing with all but which of the following HR activities?

   A. Payroll   B. Employee relations   C. Recruitment   D. Training

28. Which of the following is an example of disparate treatment?

   A. Members of a protected group are subject to stricter attendance rules.
   B. A neutral staffing practice results in discrimination against protected groups.   C. Height restrictions are set for all security guards.   D. All employees are required to take an intelligence test.

29. A team that consists of members who span functional or organizational boundaries and whose purpose is to examine complex issues such as introducing new technology, improving the quality of work processes, or encouraging cooperation between labor and management in a unionized setting is a

   A. Problem-solving team.   B. Special-purpose team.   C. Virtual team.
   D. Self-managed team.

30. Company A is referred to as top-heavy and hierarchical. What type of organizational structure best defines this company?

   A. Bureaucratic organization   B. Flat organization   C. Boundaryless organization   D. Centralized organization

31. Executive Order 11246 prohibits federal contractors and federally assisted construction contractors and subcontractors from discriminating in employment decisions if they do this amount of business a year with the government

   A. $1,000   B. $5,000   C. $10,000   D. $20,000

32. A situation in which an employer fails to use reasonable care in hiring an employee and that employee then commits a crime while in his or her position in the organization is called

   A. Due diligence.   B. Liability.   C. Negligent hiring.   D. Criminal negligence.

33. An organization that gives preference to applicants referred by current employees could be guilty of

    A. Disparate treatment. B. A historically discriminatory practice. C. Reverse discrimination. D. Intentional discrimination.

34. A method of interviewing that ensures that each interview presents exactly the same questions in the same order is a

    A. Structured interview. B. Stress interview. C. Group interview. D. Case interview.

35. This is defined as the temporary suspension or elimination of individuals' employment as a result of a business slowdown, lack of funding, or something similar.

    A. Termination B. Layoff C. Outsourcing D. Offshoring

36. Which of the following is not a legally required benefit?

    A. Health insurance B. Social security C. Unemployment D. Workers' compensation

37. This is a pay system that places most of the employees under the same compensation plan.

    A. Elitism B. Egalitarianism C. Below-market compensation D. Above-market compensation

38. An organization must set a placement goal when it

    A. Employs a smaller number of women or minorities that is indicated by their availability. B. Assigns women or minorities to jobs that are not challenging. C. Is unable to determine the ethnicity of its applicants. D. Experiences adverse impact in hiring practices.

39. The Fair Labor Standards Act of 1938 addresses all but which of the following?

    A. Minimum wage B. Gender wage discrimination C. Overtime pay D. Child labor provisions

40. This program was established as a protection of rights to employee benefits.

    A. Family and Medical Leave Act of 1993 (FMLA) B. Consolidated Omnibus Budget Reconciliation Act of 1985 (COBRA) C. Employee Retirement Income Security Act of 1974 (ERISA) D. Pension Protection Act of 2006

41. This is defined as a systematic process for gathering and analyzing information to describe jobs.

    A. Strategic analysis B. Job evaluation C. Job analysis D. Pay structures

42. When a qualified white male is denied an opportunity because preference is given to a member of a protected group, this is known as

    A. Reasonable accommodation. B. Reverse discrimination. C. Quota system. D. Undue hardship.

43. The two forms of information that are sent and received in communications are

    A. Facts and feelings. B. Personal and public. C. Implied and overt. D. Experienced and expressed.

44. This is considered one of the most important sources of information that the HR department can provide, and it sets the tone for the company's overall employee relations philosophy.

    A. Company newsletter B. Audiovisual communication C. Financial statements D. Employee handbook

45. What act includes protection against retaliation against whistle-blowers?

    A. Equal Rights Amendment of 1972 B. Sarbanes-Oxley Act of 2002 C. Fair Labor Standards Act of 1938 D. Executive Order 11246

46. Which of the following explains why employers are responsible for the discriminatory acts of their supervisors?

    A. Vicarious liability B. Hostile environment C. Quid pro quo D. Reverse discrimination

47. When an employee refuses to obey a direct order from a supervisor, it is a direct challenge of management's right to run the company. This is considered to be

    A. Misconduct. B. Poor performance. C. Insubordination. D. Delinquency.

48. The process of analyzing information about the relative worth of an employee's contributions to the organization is called

    A. Performance appraisal. B. Career development. C. Training opportunities. D. Productivity review.

49. **Which of the following is considered a voluntary separation?**

    A. Layoff **B.** Resignation **C.** Downsizing **D.** Discharge for cause

50. **The three key elements included in a job analysis are**

    A. Responsibilities, tasks, and reporting structure. **B.** Knowledge, skills, and abilities. **C.** Competencies, qualifications, and procedures. **D.** Reporting structure, pay range, and essential job functions.

51. **Generally, an organization will institute a layoff when**

    A. It cannot reduce its costs by any other means. **B.** The organization has identified low-performing employees. **C.** An employee continually receives poor performance evaluations. **D.** An employee fails an alcohol or drug screening.

52. **A human resource program that is created to help separated employees deal with the emotional stress of job loss and to provide assistance in finding a new job is**

    A. Layoff counseling. **B.** An employee assistance program. **C.** Outplacement. **D.** Unemployment.

53. **Which of the following is an appropriate response to a laid-off employee?**

    A. "It's not the end of the world." **B.** "Consider this a blessing in disguise." **C.** "It's just a job." **D.** "I can see you are upset. Is there someone I can call for you?"

54. **Outplacement firms can assist laid-off employees by**

    A. Holding mock interviews. **B.** Critiquing résumés. **C.** Both a and b. **D.** None of the above.

55. **Which of the following is not one of the major types of gain-sharing programs?**

    A. Scanlon plan **B.** Rucker plan **C.** Organoshare **D.** Improshare

56. **Which of the following is a written summary of the work to be done?**

    A. Job description **B.** Job specification **C.** Job context **D.** Job ranking

57. **Organizational characteristics that can negatively and positively influence performance are**

A. Performance factors. B. Structural factors. C. Situational factors.
D. Simultaneous factors.

58. The identification, measurement, and management of human performance in firms is known as

A. Employee coaching. B. Performance appraisal. C. Employee development.
D. Performance improvement.

59. This is the type of employee appraisal in which supervisors make judgments based on the firm's performance standards.

A. Supervisor review   B. Relative judgment   C. Absolute judgment
D. Trait appraisal

60. Which of the following is a challenge that may occur when evaluating employee performance?

A. The influence of liking   B. Organizational politics   C. Legal issues
D. All of the above

61. This is the type of employee appraisal in which supervisors compare an employee to others who do the same job.

A. Supervisor review   B. Relative judgment   C. Absolute judgment
D. Trait appraisal

62. Employees are given a chance to indicate an interest in an announced position through

A. Job posting. B. Skill tracking. C. Succession planning. D. Job analysis.

63. Which of the following is not a common type of pay for sales professionals?

A. Straight salary B. Flex-pay C. Straight commission D. A combination plan

64. Employee relationship specialists are hired to do all but which of the following?

A. Resolve grievances. B. Negotiate a labor contract. C. Provide mediation between management and unions. D. Advise top management on labor relations strategy.

65. Labor relations policy is largely based on all but which of the following acts?

A. Railroad Act of 1962 B. Wagner Act of 1935 C. Taft-Hartley Act of 1947 D. Landrum-Griffin Act of 1959

66. Which of the following is prohibited under the Wagner Act?

    A. Refusing to bargain in good faith B. Featherbedding C. Refusing to bargain with the union D. Coercing employees

67. Which of the following types of interview focuses on how the applicant handled previous situations?

    A. Stress B. Directive C. Structured D. Behavioral

68. Which of the following is not a provision of the Landrum-Griffin Act?

    A. There is a bill of rights for union members. B. A union must have a constitution. C. Unions do not need to report their financial activities to the government. D. Elections are regulated by the government.

69. Which of the following is prohibited under the Taft-Hartley Act?

    A. Interfering with employees' rights to form unions B. Discriminating against an employee who has filed charges under the act C. Refusing to bargain with the union D. Coercing employees

70. Which of the following is not one of the three phases of the labor relations process?

    A. Union organizing B. Collective bargaining C. Contract administration D. Negotiations

71. This is taking action to create and increase employees' skills to prepare them for future job opportunities and is meant to foster growth and self-improvement.

    A. Development phase B. Self-development C. Assessment phase D. Direction phase

72. A form of interview bias in which strong candidates who interview after weak ones appear more qualified is known as

    A. Cultural noise B. Negative emphasis C. Contrast effect D. The halo effect

73. Which of the following types of test measures the capacity to learn and acquire new skills?

    A. Achievement B. Aptitude C. Psychomotor D. Personality

74. Which of the following should be avoided in an offer letter?

    A. Requiring a signature on a duplicate copy of the offer letter B. Mailing employees informational brochures before they start work C. Clarifying contingencies such as a medical exam D. Quoting salary terms in an annual format

75. This focuses on providing employees with specific skills or helping them to correct deficiencies in their performance.

    A. Training B. Development C. Conduct review D. Assessment

76. This involves determining the type of career that employees want and the steps that they must take to make their career goals a reality.

    A. Development phase B. Self-development C. Assessment phase D. Direction phase

77. An ongoing organized and formalized effort that recognizes people as a vital organizational resource is

    A. Coaching. B. Career development. C. Human resource management. D. Cross-functional training.

78. In the event that unrealistic expectations are created, serious side effects of career development programs include all but which of the following?

    A. Employee dissatisfaction B. Layoffs C. Turnover D. Poor performance

79. Organizations are increasingly offering dual-career couples which of the following?

    A. Telecommuting B. Child-care services C. Flexible work schedules D. All of the above

80. This involves activities ranging from self-assessment to organizationally provided assessment.

    A. Development phase B. Self-development C. Assessment phase D. Direction phase

81. Which of the following is the main goal of training?

    A. Improvement in performance B. Enrichment and more capable workers C. Neither a or b D. Both a and b

82. The most basic reason that employees join unions is to

A. Belong to a group with similar goals and ideals. B. Help them guarantee that they have a safe, secure work environment. C. Exercise their leadership abilities. D. Fulfill their needs for self-esteem.

83. **Which of the following statements about the Taft-Hartley Act is true?**

    A. It allowed employers to file charges of unfair labor practices against unions. B. It established the NLRB to encourage growth of the union movement. C. It prohibited paycheck deduction of union dues. D. It allowed employers to establish company-sponsored labor unions.

84. **Which of the following gave union members the right to secret ballot elections for union officers and the right to sue the union?**

    A. National Labor Relations Act B. Railway Labor Act C. Labor-Management Reporting and Disclosure Act D. Labor Management Relations Act

85. **A detailed, step-by-step account of a company's customary method of handling its activities is a**

    A. Policy. B. Procedure. C. Rule. D. Vision.

86. **The *primary* reason that employee handbooks should be carefully reviewed is that they**

    A. Provide new employees with an impression of the company. B. May be the primary method of employee communication. C. May be viewed by the company's competitors. D. May create an enforceable contract.

87. **When paid union organizers infiltrate a company and begin organization efforts, this process is known as**

    A. Leafleting. B. Organizational picketing. C. Salting. D. Campaigning.

88. **Who determines whether a proposed bargaining unit is appropriate?**

    A. A mediator B. The NLRB C. Union leaders D. The employer

89. **Which of the following is usually considered a lawful practice?**

    A. Featherbedding B. Slowdowns C. Wildcat strikes D. Sympathy strikes

90. **Strikes that occur without the approval of the union leadership are called**

    A. Jurisdictional strikes. B. Wildcat strikes. C. Sympathy strikes. D. Economic strikes.

91. **Vroom's expectancy theory states that**

    A. Employees dislike rigid controls and want to accomplish something.
    B. An employee's effort is related to the Lakewood of perceived success.
    C. Employees work to meet their physical and social needs. **D.** Employees
    are likely to quit their jobs if they are treated unfairly.

92. **Which of the following is *not* a goal of orientation?**

    A. To provide remedial skills training **B.** To allow new employees to
    establish relationships with coworkers **C.** To enable new employees to
    understand company policies and procedures **D.** To permit new employees
    to gain a feeling of belonging

93. **Succession planning is based on an organization's ability to**

    A. Plan specific goals and assignments for individuals. **B.** Find candidates
    with development potential. **C.** Identify the best available candidate for
    the job. **D.** Test candidates' potential early in their careers.

94. **A job design strategy that increases the variety of responsibilities but
    requires the same skill level is referred to as**

    A. Job enlargement. **B.** Job enrichment. **C.** Job simplification. **D.** Job
    specialization.

95. **What is the value of a strong corporate culture?**

    A. It makes the maintenance of the status quo more likely. **B.** It gives
    members an organizational identity. **C.** It eliminates the need for a
    corporate ethics officer. **D.** It makes it easier for employees to question
    corporate values.

96. **Human resource strategy is made up of**

    A. Organizational resources and capabilities that help a company gain
    strategic advantage over competitors. **B.** A set of HR tactics that capitalize
    on competitive advantage for the firm as a whole. **C.** Key success factors
    in an industry that help a firm gain competitive advantage. **D.** Combining
    strategies throughout the organization and using HR tactics to gain
    competitive advantage.

97. **Which of the following is not one of the competencies required for an HR
    department to become a full strategic partner in an organization?**

A. Performance management skills B. HR technologies C. Knowledge of the business D. HR strategic thinking

98. **To foster an effective partnership between managers and the HR department, companies can**

    A. Instill a shared sense of common fate. B. View HR professionals as external consultants. C. Invite departmental leaders to participate. D. Analyze financial productivity.

99. **Which is not one of the three main reasons for complying with HR law?**

    A. It helps the company do the right thing. B. HR law sides with employers in nearly all situations. C. It allows the company to recognize the limitations of the HR and legal departments. D. Doing so limits potential liability.

100. **Disparate treatment can be defined as**

    A. Treating similarly situated employees differently because of prohibited Title VII factors. B. The effect of facially neutral policy is deleterious to a Title VII group. C. Using a screening device to weed out applicants from the pool of candidates. D. An employer having been found to have intentionally discriminated against a specific candidate for no apparent reason.

Answers to Quizzes and Final Exam

Chapter 1	Chapter 3	Chapter 5	Chapter 7
1. D	1. B	1. C	1. C
2. B	2. C	2. B	2. A
3. C	3. A	3. A	3. C
4. A	4. B	4. C	4. C
5. A	5. C	5. B	5. A
6. D	6. A	6. D	6. D
7. C	7. D	7. C	7. C
8. A	8. D	8. D	8. B
9. C	9. C	9. A	9. C
10. A	10. B	10. D	10. A

Chapter 2	Chapter 4	Chapter 6	Chapter 8
1. C	1. C	1. D	1. A
2. B	2. D	2. C	2. A
3. C	3. B	3. A	3. B
4. B	4. A	4. B	4. C
5. B	5. C	5. B	5. D
6. A	6. B	6. A	6. B
7. D	7. D	7. B	7. D
8. B	8. D	8. B	8. D
9. A	9. B	9. B	9. C
10. A	10. A	10. C	10. A

Chapter 9
1. C
2. D
3. C
4. B
5. C
6. D
7. B
8. D
9. A
10. C

Chapter 10
1. D
2. C
3. B
4. B
5. A
6. D
7. B
8. A
9. D
10. C

Chapter 11
1. C
2. A
3. D
4. B
5. C
6. C
7. C
8. C
9. D
10. A

Chapter 12
1. C
2. B
3. A

4. D
5. C
6. A
7. A
8. D
9. C
10. C

Chapter 13
1. D
2. C
3. A
4. C
5. C
6. A
7. D
8. B
9. D
10. C

Final Exam
1. D
2. D
3. C
4. A
5. C
6. C
7. C
8. A
9. C
10. C
11. A
12. B
13. A
14. D
15. D
16. C
17. B
18. C
19. A
20. C

21. B
22. C
23. D
24. B
25. A
26. C
27. B
28. A
29. B
30. A
31. C
32. C
33. B
34. A
35. B
36. A
37. B
38. A
39. B
40. C
41. C
42. B
43. C
44. D
45. B
46. A
47. C
48. A
49. B
50. B
51. A
52. C
53. D
54. C
55. C
56. A
57. C
58. B
59. C
60. D

61. B
62. A
63. B
64. C
65. A
66. C
67. D
68. C
69. D
70. D
71. A
72. C
73. B
74. D
75. A
76. D
77. B
78. D
79. D
80. C
81. A
82. B
83. A
84. C
85. B
86. D
87. C
88. B
89. D
90. B
91. B
92. A
93. C
94. A
95. B
96. B
97. A
98. A
99. B
100. A

Index